T0064697

More than Enough

Seeing Change as Blessing

Martha Westwater, SC

ARCHWAY PUBLISHING

Scripture quotations are from the Revised Standard Version of the Bible, copyright © 1946, 1952, and 1971 the Division of Christian Education of the National Council of the Churches of Christ in the United States of America. Used by permission. All rights reserved.

Interior Images:
Sisters of Charity-Halifax Archives
Mount Saint Vincent University Archives
Elaine Nolan SC

This book is a work of non-fiction. Unless otherwise noted, the author and the publisher make no explicit guarantees as to the accuracy of the information contained in this book and in some cases, names of people and places have been altered to protect their privacy.

Archway Publishing books may be ordered through booksellers or by contacting:

Archway Publishing
1663 Liberty Drive
Bloomington, IN 47403
www.archwaypublishing.com
1 (888) 242-5904

Because of the dynamic nature of the Internet, any web addresses or links contained in this book may have changed since publication and may no longer be valid. The views expressed in this work are solely those of the author and do not necessarily reflect the views of the publisher, and the publisher hereby disclaims any responsibility for them.

Any people depicted in stock imagery provided by Thinkstock are models, and such images are being used for illustrative purposes only.
Certain stock imagery © Thinkstock.

ISBN: 978-1-4808-5165-8 (sc)
ISBN: 978-1-4808-5166-5 (e)

Library of Congress Control Number: 2017953581

Print information available on the last page.

Archway Publishing rev. date: 11/13/2017

For
Sister Joanne Westwater, RGS
beloved sister, faithful religious
and for
all of my sister companions of
Sisters of Charity – Halifax

Contents

1

Marillac Residence

May 5, 2016

MAY SPRINGS FORTH IN LUSH loveliness, and I'm wondering how many more spring seasons I'll enjoy. I am now an eighty-seven-year-old Sister of Charity living in our retirement home. The other day, at the noon-time meal, someone casually mentioned *Nothing on Earth*, a book I had written in 1967. The others at table had never read it or even heard of it. The religious life described there is now considered obsolete; more often it is ridiculed. Somebody asked if I had a copy of the infamous book. Then, led by the indefatigable Sister Alice, my sisters began to urge me to write about the dramatic changes in religious life in the fifty years since that book was published and how those changes affected my life as a Sister of Charity.

As a member of the Halifax Sisters of Charity, I am proud to be one of Saint Elizabeth Ann Seton's daughters. In 1849, a little band of four sisters volunteered to leave the security of the New York foundation and brave the cold of Halifax, Nova Scotia. In 1857, seven sisters left Halifax to establish a school in St. Patrick Parish, Roxbury, Massachusetts. Later, in 1911, the sisters arrived at St. Margaret's, Dorchester.

We are a predominantly teaching order and we are slowly aging and dying. I can look back, however, on the wonderfully rich career I had as a teacher and more importantly on the blessedly happy life I have had as a Sister of Charity. From teaching grade school, then high school, I moved on to university, where my specialty was Victorian literature, but my joy was teaching Freshman English. I was a survivor of the "publish or perish" dictum with three modest books and many articles listed in my curriculum vitae.

I made up my mind to become a Sister of Charity as soon as I entered the second grade at St. Margaret's in 1935. I graduated from high school in June of 1946; World War II had ended and a spirit of triumphalism reigned. On September 8, I was accepted as a postulant; on March 19, 1947 I entered the novitiate; and on April 17, 1949, I professed my vows of poverty, chastity and obedience. Four months later I was assigned the duty of teaching the third grade at Resurrection-Ascension School in Rego Park, New York. In 1957, I packed my trunk and went to St. Veronica's School, Dorval, Quebec and then to St. Patrick's, Arvida, Quebec where I wrote *Nothing on Earth*. Let me tell you how I came to write that book.

In August 1961, I was missioned to a small convent in Arvida, Quebec, where I was to teach English literature and composition to predominantly French-speaking students. I look back with fondness on those high school students. The boys were more sexually aware than I was, and the girls had a flair for fashion that I have never seen duplicated. With a wave of a scarf or a loosening of a top blouse button, they were able to transform a dowdy two piece, green uniform to the apogee of style. I was thirty-two years old and very much unaware of the changing world.

There were six of us teaching in St. Patrick's Grammar and High School in Arvida. We knew only school-book French in a town that was 98 percent Quebecois. Newspapers and television were mostly in French. There was an English section in *L'Ingot*, the local French newspaper, but it was primarily a record of the births, marriages and deaths of the English families who held mostly administrative positions in the thriving aluminium company established by Arthur Vining Davis. On Saturdays, we'd put the television on mute and make up our own stories. We were a happy, fun-loving community, very much aware of our isolation but determined to make the most of it, both in and outside the classroom.

That was why we were out tobogganing in full habits at seven o'clock on a freezing Saguenay Valley night. The gully was very steep and, yes, we screamed, completely oblivious to standard religious decorum. Four of us piled onto that toboggan and shrieked our way to safety as we landed in a mound of heavy black clothes. No broken bones, but the noise alarmed the neighbours, who alerted the Superior. We were reprimanded.

As senior sister in the group, I was reported to the Provincial Superior, who was very kind, but made it clear that I could be doing so much more with my spare time. That was why she admonished me to do some writing. I had received the creative writing award on graduating from St. John's University in Jamaica, New York, and had just finished my master's degree in English literature at the same university. My Provincial Superior made it very clear that when she returned to Arvida the following year, she would be expecting me to have written something about religious life.

In one way, I was happy to have escaped a more severe reprimand, but in another way, I was challenged. I felt genuine affection for my students; they were serious about their work, but very much engaged in the promises of the future. Although we were still in the season of plenty, when young women were entering religious life in growing numbers, there were no religious vocations from Arvida. Perhaps I could change that.

That was the birth of *Nothing on Earth*, in which I described the progress of my own life—the first thirty-three years of it. I presented it to the Provincial. I don't know whether she read it or not, but I had fulfilled my "penance." She simply said, "Now go ahead and see if it can be published."

That June, my summer assignment was to Seton Hall High School on Long Island, New York. One morning I was doing my household charge, dusting the shelves in the library, and discovered the magazine *The Writer*, which contained a list of publishers, including the Bruce Publishing Company of Milwaukee. When I returned to Arvida, I mailed them the manuscript. It was accepted and I glowed—no actually, I was aflame—with ill-founded pride.

That pride was smothered when the Superior General read the manuscript. She was not amused and forbade its publication, chiefly because of a spitball incident I had described. It was vulgar. The book, however, was already being printed. I lost sleep—two nights of it. I called the Superior General with the news that the book was already in the process of being printed; I was then advised to bring the manuscript to a senior sister in Quebec City whose judgment was respected. Thank God Sister Camillus enjoyed the book. That was in 1967. Little did I suspect the tumultuous—cataclysmic—changes in religious life and in my own life that were to follow.

I had found deep spiritual and personal fulfilment living the vowed life of poverty, chastity and obedience, and following the daily horarium, which generally followed the routine of prayer and work established by St. Elizabeth Ann Seton.

Let me pause here to consider the vows or the evangelical counsels. I am not a theologian, and I am interpreting the vows as I have lived them. Although, these vows are interpreted by the dictates of the times in which one lives, they are rooted in Jesus's teaching in the gospel. Although Jesus never named the vows, he lived them. The vow of poverty is expressed in Mark's account of the rich young man who asked what he must do to inherit eternal life. Jesus, looking upon him with love, responded, "You lack one thing; go sell what you have, give to the poor, and you will have treasure in heaven; and come, follow me." (Mark 10:21).[1] In this passage, we find the root of religious poverty through which one renounces all money or earthly goods. For a member of my order, any earned money, cars, furniture, etc. belong to one's congregation, with the understanding that anything you need will be supplied. (Need is the operative word here.)

The second vow, obedience, lies in finding the will of God for you as you follow Jesus and those who take His place on earth, that is, congregational leaders on all levels. It means accepting assignments and going wherever there are the poor, in whatever guise poverty reveals itself.

Chastity, the third vow, is also invoked in Christ's words to the young man, whom "Jesus loved." Love is the active word here. Perhaps this is the heart of a vocation. At some point, sometimes not even recognized, a person realizes the presence of God in her own life. Faintly she hears the call, as the young man must have done when he went to Jesus seeking something beyond his temporal existence. Chastity is the giving of oneself entirely to God, body and soul. It is not denying oneself the comforting intimacy of marriage. It is a deepening of the love between oneself and God through prayer.

We were helped to live out the vows by a daily horarium. We rose at five for morning prayer and meditation followed by Mass, usually in the parish church. Then there were household duties before morning classes in the schools. Most children returned home for lunch and the sisters returned to the convent for noon prayer and lunch. Then classes resumed and around three-thirty the sisters came back to the convent for rosary, spiritual reading and quiet personal prayer before the Blessed Sacrament. A study hour was held before supper, which was followed by night prayer and another hour of study before recreation. It was a full day and those days passed swiftly and happily for the next twenty years of my life.

I received the tiniest inkling of the changes to come one day in 1959, when I was teaching grammar school in Dorval, Quebec. Sister Robert Ann and I were serving tea to a group of priests who

had just returned from Rome. We overheard their murmurs about
the coming upheaval in religious life when the number of young
people entering religious life would be cut in half. The tea servers
went into the kitchen and let out uproarious laughter. That night
we were going to the Gare de Nord in Montreal and meeting sixty
postulants who were on their way to Halifax to enter the Sisters of
Charity. But after Pope John XXIII convoked Vatican Council II,
religious life has never been the same.

It is not my intention in this book to explain religious life,
let alone justify it. Theologically, as Sandra Schneiders observes in
Finding the Treasure, "Religious life is a mystery . . . [T]he intimate
exchange between God and a human being that elicits the free
commitment of lifelong consecrated celibacy is as unfathomable as
the attraction between two people that leads to marriage."[2] Few have
so thoroughly, so comprehensively studied religious life as Sandra
Schneiders, and no one has clarified for me its essential mystery. In
this simple study I can only attempt to explore how that mystery
has been lived out in my own life, particularly in the essential part
of that life—prayer.

In thinking about mystery, I've wondered about Jesus, Son of
God and son of man. Did he ever wonder what happened to the
ten lepers he cleansed? Or what about that young man from Nain?
Did he question Lazarus about life after death or did He simply, as
Jesus from Nazareth, the ascetic, itinerant preacher, accept death's
inscrutability?

Did he ever question the voice he heard at the time of His
baptism? I used to think He knew the answers to all those questions.
But now I know that Jesus had to cope with the mysteries of human
existence just as I do. Jesus questioned God's will. He asked two
critical questions which have become the mainstay of my faith.
In Gethsemane, he asked, "Father, if it be possible, let this chalice
pass from me." And on the cross he asked, "My God, my God, why

have you forsaken me?" So now, as I write this account, I accept the inevitable place of mystery in life.

There will always be questions. When I ask myself if my particular, much loved family of the Halifax Sisters of Charity, daughters of Vincent, Louise and especially Elizabeth Ann Seton, will endure, I have to answer, judging by the lack of people entering religious life, probably not. However, I firmly believe that, although it will not continue in the way described in *Nothing on Earth*, its spirit—the love of God and service to one's neighbour made visible—will endure.

The Vatican II document on the renewal of religious life published in 1965 (Perfectae Caritatis), witnessed to *aggiornamento,* which meant simply adapting to the changed conditions of the contemporary world. Arguing that the church had been stuck in immobility for centuries, the document urged congregations to look back to their founding charism or spirit; it also encouraged us to look forward by adapting to the times. During 1965–66, I was more interested in teaching high school English and writing *Nothing on Earth* than I was in *aggiornamento*. We were being urged to test new ways of living the vowed life, but I was more interested in defending the old ways. Many of us sisters were comfortable with the familiar old ways, but the more discerning members were pressing for more personal responsibility, more freedom in the daily schedule, the use of free time, and most dramatically, changes to the religious habit.

In the early days of my religious life, we wore a long dress made of wool, with a pleated cape and apron and a coif or cap covered by a veil. In winter, we added a winter cloak with large openings for arms (and wind). In summer, we wore the same woollen habit with a lighter cloak and gloves. The habit was particularly uncomfortable in summer. I remember one sweltering hot day in New York, a sister companion and I were returning from summer school and, as usual, taking public transit. Standing on the station platform were two scantily clad women. One of them, sighting us, remarked to the other, "Look at those two nuts!" Definitely, we were not dressed for the times, nor the season.

For most apostolic congregations, the habit became associated with the romanticized stereotype of the nun. (Strictly speaking, the term "nun" applies to sisters living in a cloister; the term "religious" is reserved for those engaged in service to the church.) Around 1968–69, I unwillingly gave up the habit. I did so only because my peers were accepting secular dress. However, slowly, very slowly, I have learned the wisdom, the absolute necessity, of the changes that have taken place in religious life during my lifetime.

As I write, I realize that, according to the National Religious Vocation Conference, 90 percent of the 58,000 nuns and sisters in the United States are over 60 years-old. My congregation's numbers have decreased from almost 1,700 in the late fifties to just over 300 today. Religious sisters in general have dwindled as much as 70 percent. We no longer have a Motherhouse and we are in the process of selling land to form a Foundation that will continue the works of charity to which we have dedicated our lives. Yet, despite the diminishment, I firmly believe that God continues to call young people to serve His/Her people in love. I firmly believe that religious life will be revitalized by a new generation that is disillusioned with the corruption and greed of its political, even religious, systems and the utter materialism of its creeds. There is a growing loss of faith in the world, and a growing lack of trust in organized religion. But from this world, God continually calls young people and those not so young. From Peter and Andrew of the old Galilean world to Grace and Adelaide of the present day, that call is still active. It is for a new generation of religious sisters that I write this book.

2

575 Neilsen Street
4000 West 11 Street

St. Patrick's Convent in Arvida, Quebec was my third mission and Our Lady of Perpetual Help Convent was the fourth. It was at these two convents that I was unwillingly caught up in the vastly changing times. This was the era of John F. Kennedy and Pierre Elliot Trudeau, of anti-Vietnam protests, the civil rights movement, the quiet revolution in Quebec, the Cuban missile crisis—and the Beatles. Change seemed to be the dominant theme of the day.

When I was missioned to St. Patrick's Convent, I did not want to go. I had visited Arvida briefly when I lived in Dorval and found the place barren and cold, and the sulphur from the paper factories of Kenogomi made the air reek of rotten eggs. Even though this visit preceded the formation of the Parti Quebecois in 1968 and the October crisis of 1970—precipitated by the kidnapping and murder of Pierre LaPorte and the kidnapping of James Cross, a British diplomat—there was a decidedly antagonistic feeling between the French-speaking and English-speaking residents of Arvida.

Sometimes, when the bitterness of the outside world is accepted, as I accepted my new assignment, obedience becomes prayer. On my visit with my mother before I left for Quebec, I cried. I had always hoped that I would be missioned nearer my mother, but I never was. She died during the summer of my first year in Arvida. It was a terrible, heart-breaking loss. But I now realize that if I had not gone to Quebec, I would never have written *Nothing on Earth*, never found my interest in literature quickened, never have gone on to a happy career as a professor of English literature. In hindsight, I can see the blessed mystery of obedience. Such discoveries are usually made in prayer. May I digress here and speak briefly about my experience of prayer?

My oldest sister Agnes, long dead, gave me my first inkling of entering into union with the unseen world. One afternoon Agnes took me for a visit to the Blessed Sacrament at dear old St. Margaret's Church in Dorchester, Massachusetts. I had not yet begun school. I asked her, "Agnes, where is heaven?"

"Oh, we can't see heaven now," she replied, "but we will see it later on if we are good."

We were in the upper church of St. Margaret's and, looking around, I pointed to the pipes high above me in the choir loft. "Is heaven up there behind the pipes?," I asked. "I can't see behind *them*."

I think that was my first query about prayer, which is simply discovering the dwelling place of God. With the example of a beloved and earnestly good sister like Agnes, I have tried to never abandon my quest for the Good. After Agnes's untimely death, which left my mother heartbroken, I began going to daily Mass, and I was still determined to join the Sisters of Charity. But I had no religious experience, as I now understand it, until I was seventeen. I hesitate to write about this experience now; I have never told anyone about it even when giving spiritual direction, but I think this was my first feeling of a definite "call" to the religious life.

It was a blustering but brilliant cold day in January and I was walking to church for an afternoon visit. I remember it vividly.

I was wearing a Kelly green coat and a bright green hat with a tassel. I was visiting my Aunt Catherine who lived in Winchester, an upscale suburb of Boston. Because it was 1946, and a Sunday afternoon, there were few cars on the road. The snow banks, the extreme cold and the dazzling sunlight captured the exquisite silence of the moment. Suddenly, perhaps because of the bright sunshine, the freezing cold air and my own exhilarating good health, I felt an intense feeling of completeness, of happiness, of knowledge of the unknown, the supremely attractive unity of God. I felt such an emotional, bodily and spiritual energy, that in the midst of Highland Avenue, as the wind whipped the snow and the penetrating cold numbed my face, I stopped. I felt God's presence. More significantly, I had an intimation of the oneness of God, me and nature in the specificity of that singular moment. It was trinity in unity. The girl in the green hat had a religious experience, which has withstood all self-questioning and self-doubt.

However, as I examine it now in old age, I realize why I had never revealed it. I did not mention it when I filled out the application for entrance into the congregation. I understood then that I would be thought of as non-typical. I did not fit the stereotype. When asked why I wanted to enter, I put down the solidly simple answer, I want to save my soul and serve others. I kept my personal prayer life to myself. Indeed, we were counselled not to discuss deeply spiritual matters: "It is good to hide the secrets of the King."

In late August of 1967, as I left Arvida for a new assignment in Vancouver, my prayers were no doubt perfunctory. Point Grey, Vancouver is as different from Arvida, Quebec as one star differs from another, if not in glory, at least in atmosphere. From the freezing cold of Arvida to the lush mildness of Vancouver in 1967, I was invigorated by my change of mission. The excitement began on my Canadian Pacific train ride from Montreal to Vancouver. For the first time in my life I travelled alone—and I loved it! I had a bedsitter which transformed from a comfortable seat in the daytime to an equally comfortable bed at night. On the third day of the trip, I asked the genial porter if he would wake me early the next day so that I might see the sun rise on the Rockies. He did. I shall never forget the mystifying wonder of that occasion. I was alone in the observation car, watching the sun rise behind the mountains. I could hear the smooth symphony of the wheels, watch the sun transform those majestic mountains into a city of gold and see a lonely speck of a man in a red shirt bending over what must have been a fire. The man seemed diminished. Nature triumphed. I didn't realize it then, but that was prayer.

When I began teaching seniors at Our Lady of Perpetual High School in Point Grey, I was immediately struck by the different attitude of these students to their teachers, at least to this teacher. Somehow, they presented themselves as superior beings who were entitled to superior teaching. They had superior teaching in the sister who preceded me. I thought I could not equal her excellence and I didn't. However, in an essay contest, seven of my twelve students won trips to the Canadian Exhibition in Montreal—an exhibition celebrating one hundred years of Canadian nationhood. I felt at least I had maintained the "good teaching" reputation of my congregation.

No doubt I am mistaken, but from my time in the western part of Canada, and later when I attended a conference in California, I've thought that Canada and the United States should be divided not by their north and south positions but by their east and west similarities. People in the east, particularly people in Halifax and Boston, seem very much alike in their lack of pretentiousness, while people in Vancouver and San Diego share the same cosmopolitan sophistication. Certainly my twelve students in Grade XII English seemed more aware of the changing world, of a growing rebelliousness than I was. Their discontent and anger found expression not only in protest marches on the streets but also protests in the classroom.

There was a segment of our old rule that I took very much to heart: "They shall make their schools and academies rank among the best existing." Self-righteous being that I was, I expected students to work at their assignments as assiduously as I worked on my preparation for those assignments. It was not to be. They had a droll attitude towards deadlines. One student in particular continually asked for extensions of assignments until the number of late essays he had accumulated veered uneasily close to provincial exam time. Naturally, this student was not nearly as concerned as I about the school's performance in the provincial tests of pupils and teachers. In a final burst of anti-procrastination pique, I phoned his parents who also seemed unconcerned. His mother laughingly assured me, "We are not overly worried. Jimmy's reading and study time is more politically based. He is challenged by politics and intends to make himself a career in politics." In the battle of the free spirit (James) against unyielding resistance (me), freedom won! I don't think he ever finished those three essays, but he did pass his provincial exams, and appeared triumphant on prom night with his lovely date upon whom he smiled sweetly. He did not give the same smile to me. I later learned that he used a picture of me for dart practice. This incident was a minor shock to me. It was a rare to meet defiance in a student, but it was symptomatic of an undercurrent of rebellion that invaded the classroom during and after the Vietnam War.

The war started in 1957 and lasted until 1973. Even though it began with the participation of members of the Southeast Asia Treaty Organization, it was directed by the United States and became an increasingly unpopular war. What was most perfidious about this war was the way the military and the government lied to both the troops and the people. Drug-taking was common and morale was low among the troops. Thousands of young men called up for duty escaped to Canada. The war resulted in profound disillusionment among the young, which was compounded by the assassination of Kennedy in 1963.

That event also had a wounding effect upon the young people of Arvida, who were at this time engaged with both their own Quiet

Revolution and the separatist movement. However, the climate of discontent had not invaded the Arvida classroom—yet. Or perhaps it had invaded it and I was unaware. I do know, however, that between 1968–70, several young women from Arvida had entered the congregation, but not one persevered.

Although I sensed the rising rebelliousness of young people, I had not grasped the full significance of the changes that were taking place in society, let alone in religious life. The sixties produced a generation of countercultural, liberal activists from different national, racial, cultural, religious, educational and economic backgrounds. The changes in religious life brought about by Vatican II also seemed dramatically sudden at the time, but in hindsight it is clear that Pius XII had already begun revitalizing religious life. At the time of the First International Conference of Women Religious in 1950, he urged sisters to follow the example of their foundresses and adapt their lifestyle to meet the conditions of the present time. The Pope advised religious leaders to provide theological and professional credentials for those who would be entering the teaching, medical and social services professions. Sisters in training should be put on an equal academic and professional level with their secular counterparts. Thus came about the establishment of Juniorates, houses of continuing, sustained study, where young professed might become professionally competent.

During my year in Vancouver, I saw the effects of these changes in my own congregation, in the young sisters who had emerged from the revamped formation program, the training syllabus for young sisters. By the late sixties, these young sisters were more confident than we older members. They had their bachelor's degree before they started teaching. They were taught to think for themselves. I lived with two of these juniorate sisters at Point Grey. In some cases they were envied, criticized, ridiculed, often misunderstood. They suffered, but most prevailed.

Personally, these young sisters gave me the first evidence of the legitimacy of questioning authority. For example, one sister tearfully asked the Superior what right she had to inspect her room; another asked why couldn't she take her spiritual reading privately, as they did in the juniorate, rather than with the community. In my own mind—but coward that I was, not publicly—I too began to question authority. I owe a debt of gratitude to these younger sisters, and in the years to come that debt will be increased. It is they who will weave the wedding garment, if there is to be one, of the past and future of religious life.

These changing attitudes affected many aspects of our lives in unexpected ways. In the early sixties, we began to drive, but driving a car safely was impeded by the old, highly starched coif which obstructed vision. The habit was replaced by a modified dress, still with the long, to-the-ankles skirt, but with a simpler coif and veil. I was wearing this habit when I taught in Vancouver. It was in Vancouver that I learned to drive, but only after failing my first driving test. I never enjoyed driving, but I certainly appreciated the freedom and independence it gave me.

That summer, I received an assignment to serve as counsellor to young college students who worked at Jasper Park Lodge in Alberta—a beautiful place at any time of the year, but especially in summer. Six hundred university students would leave their college dorms to work at the lodge; they planned to save money for next year's tuition and to enjoy their freedom. But freedom and the two-fold lure of alcohol and sex made it easy to get into trouble. (There were few drugs then—none that I knew of.) Immediately after my senor class had graduated, I left for Alberta and lived at the convent adjoining a hospital that my congregation founded and still administered. This experience at Jasper opened my eyes to the changing world. Each afternoon, I went to Jasper Park Lodge, room 439, cabin j-1, where the seminarian Lyle Pedersen and I would make ourselves available for guidance and counselling. Uncertain as to how we'd meet the young people, we decided to personally deliver a memo announcing an inquiry and complaint service, as well as listing our summer offerings: Sunday evenings - McLuhan type experiences of the Christian message; Wednesday - entertainment in the Catacombs, a coffee house; Thursday - exposings which were movies, sing outs and problem hash outs. It was all non-denominational.

One particular experience at Jasper opened my eyes. I received a marriage proposal. On a lovely afternoon in early July, I was walking home when I saw an elderly gentleman sitting alone on his cabin verandah. At this time, the religious buzz words were "doing the truth in love," so I greeted the gentleman with a wave and a cheery, "Good afternoon."

He invited me to come up and sit with him awhile. I complied. He told me he was an insurance company executive and that his wife had died in the previous year. He expressed his terrible loneliness honestly and I countered with my own devastating loss of my mother. I was "doing the truth." I was not prepared for the love element. He invited me to become his wife and said we could travel around the world. He would satisfy any desire I had. I was shocked, but I knew that this was a very lonely man, not looking for marital love but only for companionship.

All I could do was to remind him that I had a vow of celibacy and that I was very happy in my vocation. I thought the matter was settled, but that night he called at the convent and repeated his offer. I was terribly worried that the Superior, or anyone else, would see me with this elderly gentleman. She didn't and I did not report the visit as I should have done. I never told anyone of that incident until a good twenty years later, but every time I see the insignia of that kind man's insurance company, I smile as I remember my one and only marriage proposal.

The summer passed quickly and at the end of August, 1968, I was on my way to Halifax. During the year in Vancouver, it had been duly noted by a visiting congregational leader that I was teaching only twelve students. As a result, after only one year in Vancouver, I was missioned to a large city high school in Halifax, Nova Scotia.

3

1094 Windsor Street

WHEN I RETURNED TO HALIFAX, I lived at the Motherhouse and taught at Saint Patrick's High School, then located at the corner of Windsor Street and Quinpool Road. The school no longer exists. I loved my students at dear old St. Patrick's. I taught English composition and literature to young women in Grades XI and XII, women with whom I've kept in touch for almost fifty years. They were among the brightest, most attentive students I have ever taught. I came back to the Motherhouse in 1967, when changes in religious life were in full swing, but, sadly, I admit I was not overly interested in these changes. I was more interested in preparing classes for my new high school assignment than I was in the Covenant of Renewal, which was being prepared for the Eleventh General Chapter of the Sisters of Charity in 1968.

The chapter's theme, Renewal for the People of God, was based on the dignity of the human person. This was the point that finally made me interested in the changes. Perhaps the greatest difference between religious life in pre-Vatican Council days and our own period lay in the emphasis given to the person. Previously, the sister existed for the congregation and the congregation for the service of the church. Today, the congregation exists for the sisters and the individual sister of the congregation for the church. As Sister Mary Olga McKenna writes in *Charity Alive,*

> [U]ntil the time of Vatican II, women religious were perhaps the most dependable but at the same time the most expendable resources in the Church on the congregational, parochial, diocesan and even global level.[3]

The new understanding of a human being as a person became the basis for a renewal of religious life, particularly in our congregation.

The dignity of the human person means that each person has a proper and unique dignity, and her rights and duties are universal and inviolable. This was an explosive idea that I did not fully understand then, but which I took very much to heart. It required one to rid oneself of the superior/inferior dialectic, restoring women to full "selfhood," freeing them from a subjugated status. So, a bit fearful of my nascent ambition, I acted on this new idea and requested permission to take a course in Victorian prose. In previous summer school courses, I had concentrated on Victorian poetry. I had written my M.A. thesis on Gerard Manley Hopkins' "The Wreck of the Deutschland," specifically the sea imagery in the poem; however, I felt I was weak on the prose of the period. I was particularly interested in John Stuart Mill's essay "On Liberty." I went to the Superior (we still used the title then), and was easily granted my request to study. Of course, my studying was to be done concurrently with my teaching, and I was left with no doubt that teaching was to be my chief priority.

In the 1969–70 academic year, I began studying at Dalhousie University in Halifax. Around this time, myself and four other sisters teaching at St. Patrick's had moved into a single family house and were experimenting in small group living. I look back with deep fondness on those sisters and the joy we took in the experiment. We were within walking distance of the school, and I was in walking distance of Dalhousie. When we lived at the Motherhouse, located in Rockingham, a bus would transport twenty of us teaching sisters to and from St. Patrick's. We all had to be ready at the exact time to board the bus. With our new living arrangement, we now had greater freedom in our use of time. We had also been accustomed to having meals prepared for us—now we could experiment with cooking, especially the evening meal. We also had complete control of housekeeping. Furthermore, we had a stipend of thirty dollars a month. We'd come a long way from those days when we were not allowed any money and were not permitted even to keep school money in our possession overnight.

Our monthly stipend was our first experience with handling personal money. This money covered clothing costs and entertainment. It was scrupulously guarded and hidden in sundry spaces. One money incident stands out with particular vividness. Of all the sisters I've ever lived with, Sister Beatrice was the kindest. She was so thoughtful of others, she often neglected herself. One day, when she was doing an errand for someone else, I thought I'd clean her room for her. I did a thorough housecleaning, even washing the windows and replacing her tattered desk cushion with a new one. She thanked me profusely, but the next day she came to me a bit shaken.

"What did you do with my cushion?," she asked.

"I pitched it, Bea. It was torn."

"Is it in the garbage?"

"Yes."

"I hid my stipend in it."

It was Friday, garbage collection day. We ran to the street and could see the giant truck turning up Windsor Street. Like two tramps, we tore through the week's debris and found the thirty dollars. Bea laughed the loudest. God bless her cheerful generous heart.

Because we were free from the tyranny of a bus schedule, we became more engaged in school activities. I coached the Reach for the Top team for St. Patrick's. This was a general knowledge competition among the area's high schools. I had five smart, highly competitive young men and women, who divided the various subjects between them, and each learned as much as each could on a given subject: literature, science, math, history, art etc. We had fun. I don't know if their general knowledge increased, but I know mine did. We made it to the finals, but lost in the last round.

I became aware of the drug culture during my St. Patrick's years. During the Lenten period of 1969, a group of senior students asked if they could have their own observance of Good Friday using the foyer of the main entrance to the school. I was duly impressed to think that religion was such an important part of their lives and that their personal faith was so deep. That Good Friday, I witnessed the foyer, dominated by a large cross, draped in purple cloth, with all of the windows covered in black. It was a sombre, silent scene with young men and women sitting on cushions and the air filled with incense.

Little did I know that on that Good Friday our students were smoking pot. Yes, times they were a-changing!

This was the time of the charismatic renewal and the youth Mass. Out went the organ; in came the guitar. Sunday evening was the time of the youth Mass, held in the auditorium of the nearby St. Vincent Guest House. Three of us sisters on Windsor Street always attended. One Sunday evening after Mass, some students and sisters were outside talking. The young people went home, but we sisters remained chatting. I saw three or five young men coming down the stairs carrying guitars and other musical instruments. I held the door open for them—only to learn the next day that the boys were not members of the youth group but local thieves who had stolen the youth group's instruments.

For me, the most significant change was in the prayer program. We attended Mass together and either the Morning or Night Prayer of the Church was recited together, but all other prayer was private. In our small community, we prayed the Evening Prayer together before the main meal. Most of us stayed with the rosary, meditation, adoration etc. but we could pray when and where we thought best for us. I rejoiced in these changes.

Another significant change was in the habit. There were three modifications to the traditional habit before most of us decided to go into secular dress. I admit that I made the change because most of the other sisters did; but I shall always remember one sister who quietly maintained the habit and wore it not only into retirement but until her dying day. My own feeling was that the world was changing too fast, but we had to be a part of that changing world. It became very clear to me that the habit was a relic of the past; we had to accept the reality of the present. Our students noticed the changes, smiled, and accepted us as we were, but for most young people in general, the wearing of the habit was irrelevant.

One other point about the era comes to mind. The students were separated by gender at St. Patrick's and the boys stayed on the boys' side and the girls on the girls' side. Ne'er the twain did meet. One noontime period, I came out of my classroom to discover a young man kissing his girlfriend on the girls' side of the building. I was absolutely shocked. Kissing? In school? Indignantly, self-righteously, I reported the deed to the school hierarchy and was told in a very Principal-like tone, that it was none of my business, which, I suppose, was the truth. These were the days of freedom and self-expression and the new buzz words were "Let it all hang out." This was one aspect of the new times that I did not want to be a part of.

4

61 East End Road

DURING THESE CRUCIAL YEARS OF transition, both in society and religious life, I found escape from the chaos of change through study. In my first year at Dalhousie, while taking a course on Victorian Prose, a professor, Dr. Clayton Myers, recommended me for a Killam Scholarship to pursue doctoral studies. Receiving it was one thing; but in 1970, I also had to receive permission to accept it. When I went to the Provincial Superior and requested permission to accept the Killam, Sister reminded me of the salary I would be relinquishing if I left St. Patrick's High School; however, true to the new thinking on the dignity of the human person, she left the final decision to me. I remember going to chapel, praying, and realizing that, yes, ambitious as I was, I did want to study, but I also felt guilty. As a Sister of Charity, all of my earnings are intended for service to the poor. Was I being selfish in relinquishing these earnings even for a year? Yes, perhaps I was, but I decided to accept both the grant and the guilt.

While still teaching at St. Patrick's, I began doctoral studies. I delighted in the personal research that graduate work entails. On weekends, I could retreat to my own study carrel in the Dalhousie library. During 1970–71, I read, read, read and re-read Victorian novels, poetry and essays. The following year I had a grant to do research on Walter Bagehot at the British Museum Library in London. It was a life-giving, life-changing experience. It was the first time I had a full year to study with no teaching responsibilities.

During this year of research, I stayed with the Good Shepherd Sisters in North Finchley, London. My own sister, Joanne, was a Good Shepherd Sister, and it was she who made the arrangements. I loved the Finchley sisters who, at this time, were light years behind us in renewal. I wore another, modern, air-force blue habit at home and wore secular dress when I took the Northern Line to Great Russell Street. Every morning, I would make a sandwich, fill my flask (thermos) with tea and walk to the East Finchley Station. Before I bought my own thermos, I could buy a cup of tea at the Museum cafeteria for two pence, about a nickel in U.S. currency. It was always steaming hot.

There is a new British Library now, but the old British Museum Library had a special, erudite aura that exuded its own particular charm. I was awe-stricken by its amazing high dome and its blue leather seats, its impressive, circular main desk, housing underneath it voluminous tomes holding information on every subject, and by its book-stacked walls, some of which revolved and became doors. The old British Library gave me a wonderful introduction to British life and manners. The English are very respectful of their eccentrics.

During my first day at the library, I noticed an elderly woman writing on a plain piece of paper. There was nothing unusual about that, but then she turned the paper and began writing over the script. Then the paper was slanted diagonally and the writing continued for hours at a time. The next day the same woman sat at the same desk and repeated the same writing pattern. This continued for a week, then a month. Finally, I asked a guard about her and was told that she was a retired, respected Egyptologist and would always be welcomed at the library. I wondered if we Americans or Canadians would show this woman the same courtesy.

Even the dear Good Shepherd Sisters were caught up in renewal, but their trial by fire was just beginning. I was able to follow our old daily prayer regimen for the most part with the English sisters— morning prayer, meditation etc., but I said my rosary walking to the train station, and I did most of my spiritual and literary readings on the Northern line, on the train running from the East Finchley to the Great Russell Street stations. I would arrive at the museum library around 9:30 and continue reading the complete works of Walter Bagehot and all of the other works on my list for the qualifying exam. I stopped work around 3:30, would take the train back to East Finchley and walk up the East End Road to the convent.

The convent's old early nineteenth-century building was surrounded by a huge wall with an equally huge wooden door, locked by a correspondingly huge key. The door was left unlocked during the day, but one night I returned home late. It was damp, rainy and a heavy fog had settled on the East End Road. Thinking of all the books I had read on crimes perpetrated on foggy London streets, I was frightened and I prayed the door would not be locked. It wasn't. A dear sister waited up for me, and when I was safe within, she locked the door. I've never forgotten the comfort of safety.

After a day at the library, I would return to the convent, change into my modern habit and go to the chapel for quiet adoration and evening prayer. I did not study at night, and during my year in London, I became addicted to British mystery novels. Ruth Rendell and P.D. James remain my favorite authors of the detective novel. I read in my room after the formal recreation period. I was quite content and moved along easily in my Bagehot research.

One delightful Good Shepherd custom was to serve a steaming cup of tea every morning to senior sisters and guests. As a guest, I certainly benefitted from this comforting luxury. Who would mind early rising?

In this year of study, 1970–71, I was not caught up in the significant congregational changes we were undergoing on the other side of the Atlantic. While I was in England, forty-one convents had closed and the number of sisters engaged in traditional ministries of teaching and nursing continued to decrease. Thus, the Twelfth General Chapter of 1972, was crucial. The theme of the chapter was Call, Response, and Mission. Sister Irene Farmer, in announcing the chapter, wrote the following:

> As Sisters of Charity we are becoming increasingly aware that our CALL is to a personal relationship with Christ; our RESPONSE is the evangelical life lived radically; and our MISSION is the duty of spreading the faith and the saving work of Christ in a constantly changing world.

At this chapter, Sister Katherine O'Toole was elected Superior General. At thirty-seven, she was the youngest General Superior ever chosen to lead the congregation. She was a remarkable woman of prayer and intelligence. Her quietly controlled leadership was a blessing. Even in 1972, it was evident that one of the greatest problems we'd face as a congregation was wrestling with balancing human freedom with the roles of authority and obedience in religious life. This was the most controversial topic of the 1972 chapter. Some felt that the principles of subsidiarity and collegiality, group government and consensus had been over-emphasized in the previous chapter and had to be redressed. Most agreed that the role of the superior general did not receive adequate attention in 1968. Authority rested in the superior general, but that authority would be severely tested by those championing individual freedom. Even as I write, the function of authority is still muddled.

Perhaps, if Sister Katherine O'Toole had lived, we would have had a balanced mind to help us through the quagmire, but Sister

Katherine, "Katie" to those who loved her, died when she was given a wrong injection during treatment for her cancer. Her death was a devastating loss to the congregation, and a personal, inspirational loss to me. Her dying wish was that no recrimination would be made. The doctor had made an honest mistake.

The call of the 1972 chapter had been to sharing the mission of the church in spreading the Good News of Jesus's teaching. Beginning with Paul VI in his Apostolic Exhortation on the Renewal of Religious Life, all religious were called to hear the cry of the poor, to reach out to help those who were oppressed, to use all means possible to heal the wounds of injustice and to leaven the world with love. We were urged to be a visible means of healing in the time in which God had placed us. Focusing on our mission made us more aware of world hunger and the world energy crisis. However, even though I did become more conscious of poverty in the world, I found my mission in preparing for my Ph.D. orals and in writing my dissertation.

5

166 Bedford Highway

UPON PASSING MY QUALIFYING EXAMS in 1972, I was appointed to the position of Lecturer in the English Department at Mount Saint Vincent University, and upon receiving my doctorate in Victorian Literature in May, 1974, I was appointed to the position of Assistant Professor. I became an Associate Professor in July 1978 and a Full Professor in 1985. These appointments describe a typical academic career; but during this period, extraordinary changes continued to be taking place in the world, in the university and in my own spiritual life.

During these years, I had to re-learn that personal and communal conversion is not a volatile matter and that the work of the Holy Spirit is always slow. One of the hardest lessons I had to learn during this period was to respect my own life experiences, particularly a woman's life experience. I had to revise my own ideas on the role of women in society.

The seventies and eighties were pivotal years in the twentieth century—especially the eighties. This was the decade when poison gas escaped in Bhopal, India, killing thousands; when the nuclear plant at Chernobyl exploded, releasing more than a hundred times the radiation of the bombs dropped on Hiroshima and Nagasaki; when Challenger exploded only seconds after lift-off; when we were warned of global warming; and when Michael Jackson was King of Pop! These events engendered a new awareness of the fragility of human life, targeting the rich and privileged as well as the poor and destitute. In this new world, even one of the most respected woman of the era, Queen Elizabeth II, could be terrified by a palace intruder (and her calls for help left unanswered); and the fairy-tale life of her daughter-in-law, the Princess of Wales, was revealed to be one of depression and loneliness. This was the era when a new world of globalism invaded the ordinary citizen's consciousness and huge concerts were held to benefit victims of poverty and disaster. The world of the eighties was a world where the dogmatism of the church and the rationalism of the civic order were severely questioned. Pierre Elliott Trudeau, Canada's Prime Minister, shook up the self-satisfied Canadian status quo. Ronald Reagan, as President of the United States, led the Reagan Revolution in economics and Margaret Thatcher, the "Iron Lady" dramatically challenged male political dominance. Saddam Hussein invaded Iran, sparking the Iran-Iraq War and Ted Turner established CNN, which attempted to satisfy a people's insatiable appetite for news.

Great changes were also taking place at Mount Saint Vincent University and the wider academic world during these years. College education was becoming increasingly accessible. We, Sisters of Charity, were very proud of "The Mount," into which previous generations of Sisters of Charity had invested their energy, time and money. In the early days, the sisters were not salaried and every sister in the congregation, from youngest to oldest, worked, fasted and prayed that the college would succeed.

The university had grown from Mount Saint Vincent College, which, in turn, had grown from Mount Saint Vincent Academy, established by the congregation in 1873 to train the teachers educating children in the public schools of Nova Scotia. In 1915, doctoral degrees were not common, especially among women, but Mother Mary Evaristus Moran, the first President of the Mount and a strict administrator, held degrees in Latin and Greek from Dalhousie, the University of London and the Catholic University of America (CUA). She firmly believed that women should have equal opportunities for education. Sister Rosaria Gorman also held a doctorate in classics from CUA, but she disliked the burden of administrative work and would have much preferred to be studying the flowers mentioned in Vergil's Aeneid. Sister Francis d'Assisi held a doctorate in history, and she was the President who led The Mount into membership in the National Conference of Canadian Universities. These sisters were among the first women in Canada to hold doctorates.

Mount Saint Vincent College took root in a twenty-year contract with Dalhousie University, established in 1915, whereby The Mount undertook to teach the first two years of the university program for the B.A. degree, the degree being granted by Dalhousie. From these early days, Mount Saint Vincent has had a long-standing, genial relationship with Dalhousie. On May 7, 1925, Mount Saint Vincent received its own charter and became the first and only women's college in Canada with power to grant its own degrees. It has had a quiet but enduring heritage. According to McKenna,

> The charter [of 1925] recognized the mother general of the congregation as the chairperson of the board, and the members of the general council as members of the board. So it was that the elected council of the Sisters of Charity exercised all the prerogatives pertaining to the college from its inception in 1925. The congregation owned the property and was responsible for the financial management of the institution and for all the sisters on faculty, regardless of seniority or degree status. The services of the sisters were contributed as an endowment to the college. [4]

Until 1951, the full-time faculty of Mount Saint Vincent College consisted solely of Sisters of Charity, and their numbers remained high until the 1960s. But times were changing. Canada was undergoing a crisis in education because of its post-World War II expansion. Around this time, a Nova Scotian, Isaac Walton Killam, left a huge legacy to the government that formed the basis for the Canada Council for the Arts, Humanities and Social Sciences. (I have benefitted enormously from Killam grants for scholarship and research.) Killam died in 1955, and the inheritance taxes on his estate amounted to fifty million dollars. The government proposed another fifty million over a ten-year period for the purpose of distributing capital grants equal to fifty percent of specific building or capital equipment projects undertaken by Canadian universities.

Mount Saint Vincent College benefitted greatly from this governmental largesse: Evaristus Hall, the academic centre, Assisi Hall, a student residence, and Rosaria, the student union building are the fruit of government aid.

By 1959, the sister faculty of the college numbered twenty-three and the full-time lay faculty eight, five of whom were male. However, The Mount clung to its original goal: the education and advancement of women. Perhaps the greatest expansion in The Mount's history took place under Sister Alice Michael Wallace, whose installation on March 19, 1966 was a very formal affair at which the sister faculty wore academic attire for the first time. In less than a month, on April 6, 1966, the Nova Scotia Legislature granted a new charter that changed the name and status of Mount Saint Vincent College to Mount Saint Vincent University. The Mount had come of age. It was Sister Alice Michael who appointed me to the English Department of Mount Saint Vincent University.

Just as The Mount had grown in academic achievement, so had its dedication to the advancement of women expanded. The whole world order changes dramatically when the position of women changes, and our position as women in the congregation was changing rapidly. At this time, during the eighties, we were experimenting with the new, ever flourishing freedom granted us by the congregation. That freedom was based on those principles set down in the 1968 chapter of renewal: respect for the human person, subsidiarity and collegiality. We also recognized that, given all this freedom, many were leaving the congregation and few were entering. One to leave was the remarkable Sister Alice Michael Wallace.

At this time, I lived on the eighth floor of Assisi Hall, the women's dorm. The Student Union had been revitalized and was a dominant force at the university. Students demanded their own watering hole—alcohol at The Mount! Unthinkable!! At that time, we sisters were still under the delusion that our role as sisters in the college was to act in loco parentis. That idea was fading fast just as Vinnie's Pub came into existence. The pub was open on certain nights, and the girls revelled in their new freedom.

One event stands out in my mind. The girls would often leave campus after Vinnie's closed and continue carousing at pubs in the city. One night they came home around three in the morning, making a terrible racket. I peeked out of my room to see about six girls wheel-barrelling one another to their rooms. It was a comical sight, but it was not so funny when my alarm went off later at five. I had had it!

At six, I began phoning, from my room in residence to the eighth-floor common-use phone and asking for Jeanine, disguising my voice as a man and claiming she stole my wallet. The first girl to answer politely informed me that Jeanine was sick. I called regularly all through the day making the same claim. At lunch period one girl came to my office claiming Jeanine was receiving "crank" calls. By five, the calls were labelled "obscene." When I returned to the dorm after an evening class, the girls met me with the report that Jeanine was hysterical. I sat by Jeanine's bed, like a good old Dutch uncle, and found out all about the "fun" they had the night before, going to the Misty Moon, a night club in the city. Jeanine was scared and

I should have been! But I assured Jeanine that if the pervert called again, someone should notify me. Of course, the self-made call came and I assured the "pervert" that the police had been contacted and he was not to call this number again.

I had remedied a bad situation, and to this day those young women, some of whom are now grandmothers, never knew the identity of that mysterious caller. I was learning fast though. Times had changed and I had better learn that these students were not "girls" now; they were "women." And I had to change my thinking about women.

I had always believed that a woman was equal to a man intellectually if not physically. I also maintained that women achieved more academically when educated by gender. At the same time, I think I had submitted into believing that a woman's chief role was as a nurturer, and that, as the daughter of Eve, she was always in danger of luring Adam into sin. Myth is a powerful embodiment of mystery.

Because most literature on the spiritual life was written by men, my thinking at the time emphasized reason, the mind. Emotions, feelings were the demands of the "self," and the self was to be feared, denied; however, too much denial can lead to a hardness of heart. I think my heart was hardening. Although religious no longer practiced self-humiliation by publicly admitting infractions of the rule and asking for penances, I still believed that the body had to be disciplined, natural desires modified, if not repressed. But feminist religious like Sister Joan Chittister were making me acknowledge the dominant role men had in the formation of religious women. As she wrote in *The Fire in These Ashes*, "Men knew that what they could not control in themselves they needed to control in others. The solution became the eternal subservience of women."[5]

In the years following Vatican II, particularly in the eighties, I began to understand that the body was not the enemy. I was beginning to appreciate the interconnectedness between body and soul; between my natural and my spiritual selves. I was also beginning to learn that, though in heaven there might be no distinction between male and female, on earth there was certainly plenty of it. Mount Saint Vincent University would hold tenaciously to its founding goal—the education of women.

To a greater or less degree, I was becoming a budding feminist, throwing off the yoke of male domination. This was evident in my attitude towards authority. No longer was the will of the Superior accepted as the will of God; rather, I, as an individual, was expected to find God's will in prayer, in discernment and in consultation with our Superior (congregational contact person). But even the idea of a Superior was becoming outmoded. Most of us were now happily electing our coordinators.

My own embracing of the feminist movement came from my research, particularly research on one upper-class woman in Victorian society who became as much a victim of her class as lower-class women were victims of theirs. Norman St. John-Stevas, later raised to the peerage as Lord Fawsley, had given me access to the diaries of Walter Bagehot's wife. In transcribing these dull diaries, I was struck by the idea that this intelligent woman, who was the daughter of James Wilson, the founder of *The Economist,* and the wife of Walter Bagehot, perhaps the most brilliant journalist of his day, was unable to overthrow the traditional assumptions of women's role; her duty was "to contribute daily and hourly to the comfort of husbands, of parents, of brothers and sisters in the intercourse of domestic life."[6] The constant refrain in Eliza Wilson Bagehot's diaries was, "Upstairs with headache." She had retreated from her restricted life.

I rejoiced at and took part in The Mount's dedication to the education of women, especially during the seventies and eighties, when it made a decided push to entice older women back to college by establishing the Women's Studies program and providing child care facilities for the children of working women who wanted to attend university. I was exhilarated by The Mount's championing of women's rights!

There were other events that I connect with my first years at Mount Saint Vincent. The first was my first publication and the second was my long retreat.

After finishing my studies, I condensed a chapter in my dissertation and submitted an essay "Walter Bagehot: A Reassessment" and submitted it to a journal for publication. It was rejected. I was reading the rejection letter in the faculty lounge when one of my colleagues in the English department commented on my dejected look. I simply told him that I just received a rejection letter. "Oh," he replied, "I paste all my rejection letters on my wall. Just iron it out and re-submit it." I took him literally—went home, took out the ironing board, ironed out the wrinkles in the manuscript and submitted it again. It was accepted by the *Antioch Review* and appeared in the Winter issue (1977) of that journal. Naiveté sometimes brings strange rewards. But it was my thirty-day retreat that was the most important event of my life at the time. It requires special treatment.

6

Mabou

IN A SMALL CONVENT ATOP a gentle hill, in a lovely bucolic setting, and within walking distance of the mighty Atlantic, I made my thirty-day retreat during the month of July, 1975. My studies were completed and I was settled at the university, so now I could take a long, lingering examination of my prayer life. I was looking forward to a quiet, restful time with the Lord. There would be leisurely walks in the countryside watching the cows grazing in the fields, refreshing swims in the July heat and loving conversations with my God. It was not to be as easy as I thought.

Satisfied that I had not neglected prayer during my years of study, I went confidently into retreat. I had asked for a Jesuit retreat director. Instead, I was given a diminutive sister of the Congregation of Notre Dame. In the *Exercises,* St. Ignatius advises that the retreat director of a long retreat "should permit the Creator to deal directly with the creature, and the creature with his Creator and Lord."[7] Sister Margaret did just that as she presented the first principle and foundation of the exercises: Man is created to praise reverence, and serve God our Lord, and by this means to save his soul. "Hmm," said I to myself, "I learned that lesson in the first grade catechism which asked, 'Why did God make you?'" The answer was the same, "God made me to know, love and serve Him in this world and to be happy with Him in the next." What was new about this First Principle, the foundation of the spiritual exercises?

During the first week, I followed the strict regimen of prayer, which consisted of five hours of meditation and contemplation, one hour to be taken at midnight. I thought the last mentioned time meant at twelve a.m., only to be told that that period of prayer was to be taken in the middle of one's nightly sleep (mid-night), which for me was three in the morning. I switched my prayer to the appointed hour and was surprised to find other retreatants in the chapel at the same time. I was comforted by their presence.

The first point of the first meditation calls for one to use one's memory, understanding and will to recall the fall of the angels. That was easy. I thought of Milton's *Paradise Lost* and Lucifer's proud, "Non serviam," and that other memorable line: "Better to reign in hell than serve in heaven."[8] Yes, Lucifer was proud and disobedient, but of course, there really was no similarity between Lucifer and me! Yes, I am proud, perhaps I am arrogant, but I'm doing my best to put down the dogs of self-approval. I am trying to serve the Lord here on earth. I am no Lucifer.

In the second point of the first week's meditation, the retreatant is asked to apply all the powers of the soul—memory, understanding and will—to consider the sin of Adam and Eve. After being placed in the Garden of Eden, they were forbidden to eat the fruit of the tree of knowledge. They disobeyed, and were thereafter clothed in garments of skin and cast out of Paradise.

Adam's was the sin of disobedience. Oh, this was an easy meditation. I was not like Adam. Didn't I go to Arvida without complaint, heartbroken though I had been? I have been obedient most of my life.

The third point asks the retreatant to apply her three powers to the person who went to hell because of one mortal sin. Had I committed a grave sin? This is where I came up with my first line of defense: I have never hurt anyone intentionally.

There you have the meditations and contemplations for the first week. For three days I meditated on the first sin of Lucifer, then that of Adam and Eve and then on personal sin. For the following three days, I was to meditate on the punishment due to sin. Every morning I would go to my retreat director, the gentle Sister Margaret, and recount my periods of prayer. The first seven days passed peacefully enough, and I did not tell my patient listener that I had accepted the fall of the angels and of Adam and Eve as myths that reveal the truth about man's inescapable sin of pride. However, my sin was taking to myself the credit for graces and gifts received. By the tenth day of the retreat, I was sick and tired of sin and I asked when I could go on to the meditations on the life of Christ. She sent me back to the meditations on the fall of the angels, the disobedience of Adam and Eve and personal sin.

On the tenth day, I was angry. Very, very angry that Sister Margaret would not let me go beyond sin and contemplate the life of Christ. I masked my anger during the interview and accepted Sister Margaret's word that I continue contemplating sin; I did this sweetly, even with a smile. However, when I returned to my room, I exploded. "What the hell did a man from the seventeenth century know about a woman religious of the twentieth century???" So furious was I that I swore aloud and threw Puhl's edition of *The Spiritual Exercises of St. Ignatius* against the wall. It was a forceful pitch and the binding cracked.

At that very moment, I heard the pitiful, aching wail of a cow who had just had her young calf removed. With that cry, I too cried, "Why am I so angry? What is wrong with me?" I fell to my knees and sobbed, but in those moments I think I finally understood personal sin—the sin of Satan, Adam and Eve, and me. I had refused to accept my creaturehood. All sin is a denial of creaturehood. I acknowledged my rejection of my creatureliness in my will for power.

Constricted though it might be, I understood that I wanted to be in control of my life. I was/am a self-righteous prig. What a breakthrough that understanding was even though, as I write, it looks so simple, so elementary. When I acknowledge my own creaturehood, I have to embrace all the sins of humanity. I am part of all the evil in the world.

This recognition of my complete dependence on God is the source of my union with Him and with all humankind. The emphasis is on God. So bound up was I in study and success that I had ceased to make God the genuine centre of my life. In my life, the ego reigned; in the God-centred soul, everything outside of God is a matter of indifference. That is what constituted my creaturehood; my utter need of God, accepting God as Master and finding the mystery of God in my human experience. The revelation that all human beings are creatures of God makes us look anew on all those people with whom we associate in this our life.

I found the best expression of this discovery of my core self and the hidden Godhead in others in Hopkins' poem, "As Kingfishers Catch Fire." He writes in the last four lines of the octet:

Each mortal thing does one thing and the same:
Deals out that being indoors each one dwells;
Selves – goes itself *myself it speaks and spells*,
Crying *What I do is me: for that I came.*

Each self is unique. My self is unique, a creature made by God with all its beauties and its imperfections. I must surrender that self to the God who is its centre. Complete union demands obedience to God's will as it unfolds in the everyday events of life. Just as the old cow was emptied of her calf, so must I be emptied of self-centredness and become other-directed; because the God who lives in me lives in all his people. The God of Mystery is my "indoors being" and when, and if, I can find that "indoors being" in others, then I have found the mysticism of the Christian life. As Hopkins writes in the last four lines of the poem's sextet, each person,

> Acts in God's eye what in God's eye he is –
> Christ – for Christ plays in ten thousand places,
> Lovely in limbs, and lovely in eyes not his
> To the Father through the features of men's faces.

When I returned to Sister Margaret the next day, I knew I had been blessed. I told her what had happened, how I questioned the source of my anger and the pain in discovering my sinfulness in the cry of a cow.

My retreat at Mabou, Nova Scotia, changed my life, but I did not yet fully understand the emptying of self that surrender to God entails.

7

5l Marlwood Drive

IN 1976, AFTER HAVING BEEN interviewed and assessed, I was accepted into the Sisters of Charity community at 51 Marlwood Drive, Halifax, Nova Scotia. The house itself bespoke brightness and openness. Entering the front door, across the small foyer, you could look into the parlor and see a welcoming wooden rocker, a large picture window overlooking natural woodland and a magnificent, proud Boston ivy plant on an equally stately stand. We five Sisters of Charity (I'll use our own names), Gerry, Betty, Yvonne, Sheilagh and I, all taught various strands of human knowledge at the University: Biology, American Literature, British Literature, Math Education and Theology. We were a mixed group from Boston, New York, Halifax and Newfoundland. We were perhaps more interested in our own disciplines than we were in the affairs of the world, but we were all very conscious of the changes that were taking place in the world, particularly the changes in the congregation.

I was older than the others, and I think they were wary of my conservative leanings, but my years at Marlwood might well have been the happiest of my religious life. My professional life flourished, my spiritual life deepened and so did my love of the congregation.

Perhaps most importantly, these years led me to a new understanding of the necessity of change in religious life.

It was also a time of changes in the university. Once the college achieved the status of a university, there were higher standards of scholarship demanded. The salaries of the Sisters of Charity were still considered "contributed services," and teaching was still the prime duty of professors, but more stress was now placed on publication. I was fortunate to have arrived at The Mount at this time, as the academic publish-or-perish dictum challenged me to explore new areas of thought. This academic research also helped me to grow in understanding the changes in religious life.

Thanks to Canada Council grants, during my years at Marlwood I was able to publish three books that answered three significant (at least for me) questions. In my first research project, which resulted in the publication of *The Wilson Sisters: A Biographical Study of Upper Middle Class Victorian Life*,[9] I asked myself, "Why would six upper-middle-class women like the Wilson sisters be in total opposition to extending the suffrage to women?" The simple answer was that they were hostages to uncertainty. They feared the loss of a ritualized society in which each woman and all her actions had ordered meaning. The Wilson sisters' confidence rested on position not personhood. As part of the rising middle class, they were confident of their father's prestige in business and in Parliament, but they could never feel the same confidence in themselves.

My research for this book required transcribing the diaries of Eliza Wilson Bagehot. Eliza kept a diary from 1851, when she was eighteen, until her death in 1921. From the outset it was the dullness of the diaries that piqued my curiosity and sent me back time and time again to the eight-year task of transcribing that horribly cramped, spidery handwriting which chronicled the lives of six women who endorsed the Anti-Suffrage Manifesto of 1889.

The Wilson sisters' fear of losing their places in a ritualized social pattern mirrored my own fear of letting go of the externals of religious life: the habit, the ceremonial life of the daily horarium, the fear of losing place as a privileged member of the church. Like them, I clung to the emphasis on position not personhood. The publication of this first book was celebrated at a delightful supper given by Norman St. John-Stevas at his home in Knightsbridge. This book received more critical attention than any of my other books, and my joy was heightened because my own Sister Mary Olga McKenna was studying in London at this time and was able to celebrate this occasion with me.

My second book answered the question, "Why are some of the strongest, most creative minds bewildered at times into incapability, dullness, inertia? Why do some brilliant minds sink without trace while others, less brilliant, succeed?" In *The Spasmodic Career of Sydney Dobell*,[10] I argued that Dobell's major work *Balder* might well be labelled feminist, because his depiction of male cruelty and arrogance exalted women's sensibility and made it distinctly superior to men's. Balder was ridiculed by William Aytoun, and Dobell was victimized by an egotistical, male dominated publishing industry. In researching his book, I became more aware of the compelling ambivalence of feminist studies and how religious women were victimized by a male-dominated clergy. *The Spasmodic Career of Sydney Dobell* did not garner the same reviews as *The Wilson Sisters*, but based on the research, I was asked to contribute several entries to the *Dictionary of National Biography*.

My last book was *Giant Despair Meets Hopeful: Kristevan Readings in Adolescent Fiction*.[11] It had an interesting conception. In the autumn of 1989, I was riding British Rail from London to Westbury. In the same compartment, a group of teenage American exchange students were travelling with their teachers to Stonehenge. The three-thousand-year old mystery of that circle of stones had already exercised its magnetism on at least one of the students, for in a rare moment of quiet, a young American queried in a raw, clear, mid-western voice,

"Sir, do you believe in God?"

"No," was the quiet, laconic English master's answer. "Do you?"

"I don't know about God, but I sure as hell believe in the devil," was the student's firm reply.

The belief in a supernatural force that had inspired men to haul fifty-ton monoliths of stone twenty-four miles over the Marlborough Down to Stonehenge still exerts its transcendental power. So does the glorious four-hundred foot spire of nearby Salisbury Cathedral, uttering its sublime prayer in stone to the Christian God who has dominated European civilization for over two thousand years. But for this young man, still a boy, the force of evil exerted more power. Why was evil more attractive, more seductive than good? Why was the father figure disappearing from adolescent fiction? Why would one participant at a conference on children's literature voice the stark opinion that the sooner we got rid of the idea of the family, the better off society would be? I was becoming aware that not only were changes, big changes, taking place in religious life, they were also taking place in young people's lives. Childhood was shrinking; young adulthood was expanding.

In the eight years between that train ride from London to the south of England and the publication of my third book, I traveled on three continents; from Ayers Rock, sacred to indigenous Australians, to the Parisian apartment of Julia Kristeva, I was nourished by the imaginative wisdom of the several writers of the sixties and seventies whose works I explored. I used Julia Kristeva's contention that adolescence mirrors the malaise of our society. In her essay "The Adolescent Novel" she describes the adolescent as a mythic figure whom we create in order to distance ourselves from our deficiencies by projecting them onto someone who has not yet grown up; she forces us to confront the perpetual adolescence in ourselves.[12] Kristeva helped me view suffering in the lives of all, youth and adult, as a splinter of the divine idea. Research for this book was personally satisfying, as it allowed me to meet great writers who were also beautiful human beings.

I turned fifty at Marlwood, and I think the years between fifty and seventy were the most fruitful of my life. Along with the excitement of new ideas, I was learning to appreciate the value of living in a community of women who were essentially good. It was from the community at Marlwood that I was given the example of how the principles of renewal, which fostered the changes in religious life, could be lived. Those principles were laid down at the Chapter of Renewal of 1968.

The dignity of the human person: Each person has a proper and unique dignity and his/her rights and duties are universal and inviolable. Certainly, my long retreat had made me appreciate the uniqueness of others.

Subsidiarity: Decisions pertaining to the government of the congregation should be made and carried out at the level of responsibility appropriate to the body in question. Superiors at every level should be given autonomy to make the decisions pertaining to their own provincial or local communities.

Collegiality: Based on the principle of shared responsibility, all members should participate in governing and obeying.

These three principles gave birth to a totally new way of living; it was to have a profound effect on me personally at 51 Marlwood Drive because the sisters living there, different in personality and temperament as they were, tried to make these principles live. Recognizing the dignity of the human person helped me understand individual differences. Let me give you an example of how I was learning to live out this principle. I say "learning" because I was still thinking I was in control of things. I was (and still am) judgmental, always thinking my way is the best.

One early morning in the January of my third year as a member of the Marlwood community, I came into the kitchen to see a sister making toast while the oven was set at 450°F and the oven door opened. I was shocked at the waste of heat—and the cost. "Hey," I cried, "You left the oven door open." "I know," she replied, "I'm freezing." In my mind, I thought of the waste of electricity and the cost. I was passing judgment on her observance of poverty. I did not acknowledge differences between her position and mine. She lived on the bottom floor in a corner room where she caught the cold wind from every direction. I lived upstairs in a brighter, warmer room. She must have been freezing down there and sought a bit of comfort in a kitchen's warmth. Here I was judging her. I was learning to live out the meaning of respect for the human person, no matter what the differences may be.

The principal of subsidiarity rests on the meaning of "subside"— to sink to the bottom. In this principle, we sought to obliterate the distinction between superior and inferior. I became very much aware of the meaning of this word very early in the first month of my residence at Marlwood. Usually on Labour Day, at the beginning of the September term, the community would picnic at a nearby provincial park and during the picnic we would elect a new coordinator and establish our aims and objectives for the year. We would picnic first, have a short prayer and then we would elect our coordinator (the old name for a superior), someone to be "in charge" for the following year. Usually we took turns holding this office. We established our aim: to live in love and peace so that we could fulfil our mission as educators at Mount Saint Vincent University. Then we would discuss our failings as a community. We were honest in these sessions—perhaps because they were conducted in open country, usually in the woods or by the ocean, we could admit our faults and then establish our objectives, for example, to be more hospitable and to invite colleagues who had no family or whose family lived afar to holiday meals.

At this meeting, we would divide chores for the upkeep of the house, each taking responsibility for shopping, preparing meals, cleaning etc. Budget concerns were also raised. Should we install cupboards in the laundry? Did we need them? How much would they cost? In this way, everyone participated and we did try to live the principle of collegiality.

Another profound change in this period of renewal was that prayer became personal. When possible we attended Mass as a community, but our different teaching schedules made any settled time for communal prayer very difficult. Formal Morning and Night Prayer, as was practiced assiduously in the old dispensation, had now been replaced by personal prayer. Although in the past, seeing my sisters assembled at five-thirty in the morning for prayer had been a great aid to my own prayer, now daily prayer was completely private. I thought that we were now more in keeping with Jesus' injunction, "But when you pray, go into your room and shut the door and pray to your Father who is in secret; and your Father who sees in secret will reward you." (Matt. 6:6). I think this passage is at the heart of the entire renewal experience.

The house was always silent in the early morning. Only around eight did the house come alive again for another day. However, the kindness and consideration of others that characterized the spirit in the house made me feel that ours was a praying community. Different though our prayers might be, prayer was the spiritual energy that gave life to the house.

Another form of prayer recommended by Ignatius is the daily examen of conscience, the centuries old custom of assessing progress or regression in one's spiritual life. In the old dispensation, I had a little, black, paper-covered book and pencil which advised, at the beginning, with no explanation, "Imagine you are on Calvary in the presence of your Crucified Jesus." At seven o'clock in the evening, sometimes much later, I could very rarely put myself in the presence of my crucified Jesus. Prayer demands concentration as well as imagination. I am a morning person; at night I have limited power of concentration. Any prayer I make, or significant work I do, is usually done best before noon. I rarely succeeded in putting myself in the presence of Jesus. If, at evening prayer, I tried to imagine myself kneeling down at the foot of the cross, I'd fall asleep. My examen then consisted in marking, sometimes perfunctorily, how many times I broke silence or spoke unkindly—whatever the fault or sin I was trying to overcome at the time. The examen centred on myself.

In contrast, the new practice of the Awareness Examen advised relaxation in the Lord's presence, quiet reflection on the events of the day; listening to the Lord where he was meeting, challenging, being present during the day. Just letting the corks of persons and events pop to the surface of one's mind so that one could recognize Christ in them. The examen had shifted from being self-centred to being Christ-centred. It demanded a faith deeper than what I had.

Faith. How can I describe my faith, as it is so often riddled with doubt? Even in practicing the examen or in the most exalted moments of prayer, I might be assailed by doubt. I remember in the novitiate going to my dear Sister Margaret Therese and weeping that I no longer believed in Christ in the Eucharist. Wise woman that she was, she simply said, "It will pass. The devil is real." Next morning I found in my desk a little note in Sister Margaret's handwriting, in which she quoted Tennyson:

Tears, Idle Tears
I know not what they mean,
Tears from the depths of some divine despair…

The words "divine despair" have lingered in my memory. Is doubt our divine despair? I didn't recognize then that the lines were from Tennyson's poem of the same title, but later in studying "In Memoriam," I came across the lines, "There lives more faith in honest doubt,/Believe me, than in half the creeds" (XCVI). These lines have always assured me of doubt's necessity, part of our divine despair. They have given me, and countless others to whom I've quoted them, immense peace.

From my sisters at Marlwood and my colleagues at the university, I learned the power of example. In the English department, for instance, Peter was the one with ideas. As a Yale man, he was light years ahead of me in dealing with the younger generation. He was the founding father of the English Society at The Mount. It was the English Society that sponsored the "Oscar Wilde Memorial Croquet" and the Medieval Banquet. I look back fondly on Peter, who taught me so much about how to deal with a new generation. And also on David who set me on the path to publication and on John who could make the one word—BIG—encompass the greatness of Milton's *Paradise Lost*, and on Olga, Renate, Susan and dear Anna who brought me up to date on the position of women in modern society. These people enlarged my vision and made my career at The Mount successful and enjoyable.

There is one other aspect of my life at Marlwood that I credit to my colleagues at Mount Saint Vincent University. My teaching improved. I learned different ways of approaching literature. The English Department had introduced a new Freshman English program. We still used the old *Norton Anthology of English Literature*, but the Freshman class of 120–150 students was divided into two groups with class times at either 9 or 11 a.m.

Freshman were free to choose either time slot, during which there were lectures from four professors and tutorials from one. In these tutorials, limited to no more than fifteen students, essay topics were assigned and corrected and grades were distributed. We team-taught the lectures, so I witnessed a variety of teaching styles from the dramatic to the laid back. I benefitted enormously from this experiment. I have to classify my own style as one of the more dramatic approaches to teaching literature. I still love to teach the power of defiance in Edmund's speech in *King Lear*, with its infamous but powerful, "... I grow; I prosper:/ Now, gods, stand up for bastards."[13] And the opening lines of Hopkins' *The Wreck of the Deutschland*: "Thou mastering me/ God! giver of breath and bread;/ World's strand, sway of the sea;/ Lord of the living and the dead";[14] Such contrasting emotions and ideas! How expressive of life!

In 1988, the Sisters of Charity at 51 Marlwood Drive found themselves adrift in a new world order where money meant power, and education came more and more under the control of government. Those of us who had begun our degree work at The Mount and had prided ourselves on our work in education had to abandon the college. In 1988, the Sisters of Charity relinquished ownership of Mount Saint Vincent University. It was heartbreaking. Six years later there was another heartbreak: I reached the compulsory retirement age of sixty-five.

In 1994, I cleared out my office and said goodbye to students whose youth, goodness and energy always uplifted me and to colleagues who were also friends. I left behind my books, a good copy of Van Gogh's "Sunflowers" and many, many, happy memories. There were two or three unhappy ones, but they faded in comparison to the joys I had at Mount Saint Vincent University. I was disconsolate at leaving. The gift of prayer kept me from despair.

In prayer we respond to God's invitation: "The Spirit and the Bride say 'Come'." (Revelations 17). Let everyone who listens answer "I come." All who want it may have the water of life. I possessed the water of life whenever I made the effort to contact the God within. Not that I had deep feeling in prayer. I didn't. More often I was conscious of the dry, dusty soil of my heart. These were *De Profundis* days when I prayed "Out of the depths, Lord, I cry to you for help." (Psalm 130). There were other days when I thought I might get lost in my own dark hole of ambition. I knew I needed the water of life, which meant simply to know that only the Lord's presence within could make me happy. So even though I had to detach myself from the riches of university life, I was given the grace to know that the Holy Spirit would come into my life in a totally new way.

In my penultimate year at the university, I received the Excellence in Teaching Award. Nothing could have pleased me more. I stayed one more year at Marlwood, but left to live in the city. I had decided to work with the poor.

8

2551 Beech Street

WE NO LONGER OWN THE Beech Street House, and I wonder about the sunflowers I planted at the back garden wall (very small garden, indeed, and a rather ugly fence), but my years at Beech Street were the most difficult of my life. I volunteered to be communications director for the congregation—an office which, at that time, consisted chiefly of writing a monthly newsletter *Changing Times* and the obituaries for the sisters who had died. The house I lived in was a two-family affair converted into one. Three of us lived there. It was very different from Marlwood, but I had the incomparable consolation of living with two dedicated Sisters of Charity, Maria and Maureen.

With Maureen I shared a love of teaching and of literature. She was a skilled teacher of students of any age, and long after she retired, she still taught immigrant families. Maria, a splendid clinical psychologist with incisive intellectual abilities, had a private practice in addition to being heavily involved in congregational business.

I started a teaching program, MAET (Mothers Advanced Education Team) at a Dartmouth housing development, ably assisted by Sister Maureen. We shared many laughs together at this venture.

Maureen and I, with a few volunteers, had the use of a six-room house where we taught English speaking and writing skills and also a program in which students could earn a G.E.D. I remember with fondness several adult students like Josephine, Diane, Leslie and Debbie, but I also remember one day, at lunchtime, walking through the project and crying. I missed the university, although I still taught a night course in Children's Literature there.

My chief outlet during this period was in housecleaning the "after-school house." How I cleaned that single family house, using bleach, lots of it, to prevent germs spreading! But it came alive during the day, when the children trooped in for cookies and milk and help with homework.

Soon, however, I was to have a truly life-changing experience. I still remember even the smallest detail of that life-transforming event. I shall always associate the accident with my time at Beech Street.

It was at five-thirty in the grey dawn of October 9, 1998, that I left my home on Beech Street in the heart of Halifax to pick up Sister Agatha Vienneau, who was staying at our Mount Saint Vincent Motherhouse, located on a high hill overlooking the majestic, mysterious Bedford Basin. We were to begin a journey that was intended to take us to Biddeford in Maine, the site of our cluster meeting. Clusters were small groups that had been formed after the 1996 chapter. As communities were diminishing in numbers and many sisters were living alone, clusters were formed to preserve community bonding.

That grey October morning, I remember driving peacefully along the Bedford Highway where the lights from the container ship port cast a yellowish, mellow glow on the calm waters of the Basin. There were very few cars on the road. As I turned up Seton Road, which leads to the Motherhouse entrance, I realized I was five minutes early to pick up Agatha. But Agatha of the beaming smile was already waiting for me in the foyer and came through the doors carrying her one suitcase. Agatha was a last-minute change to our passenger list. Her would-be companion, Sister Paule from Bathurst had been stricken with the flu so Agatha drove to Halifax to meet Betty and me. I embraced her warmly. I had known Agatha for over fifty years and loved her winning, shy smile, her gentle ways, her quiet sense of humour and her honesty. Agatha was not one to venture an opinion unsolicited, but when asked, her replies were straightforward and directed to the heart of the matter. I packed Agatha's suitcase in the trunk beside my own, offered her the passenger seat, and then went to pick up Sister Elizabeth Bellefontaine, who was still living at Marlwood.

As I drove up to Betty's house in the much-loved, quiet sub-division on the outskirts of the city, I could see her in the kitchen window making tea. She was standing at the sink, under a large bay window facing the road, pouring water from a kettle into her thermos. (Betty's tea always had to be scalding—weak but scalding.) A few minutes later the kitchen light went out, the hall light came on. Then Betty put on her coat, shut off the light and came out her front door. She would never enter that door again. I helped Betty store her suitcase and garment bag in the trunk and she took the seat behind Agatha in the rear of the car.

We were a very happy threesome leaving for Biddeford that grey morning. As the daylight increased, we knew rain was forecast but nothing seemed to dampen our spirits. We began our journey with a prayer: "Along the way of peace and prosperity, may the Almighty Lord lead us. Our Lady of the Highways, guide and protect us." We were chattering about the many changes in the passenger list. Sister Helen was to come with Betty and me, but she decided at the last minute to travel in the car that was to take two days to complete the journey. Betty had asked Sister Pat if she would like to drive with us, but Pat felt too tired and decided to fly. Agatha told her story of reversed plans and we laughed at the typicality of nuns' transposed travelling patterns but congratulated ourselves that we three were so congenial and compatible a group. The bright chattering simmered into quiet once Betty suggested we take time for morning prayer and meditation. We were travelling in harmony and peace.

About an hour later Betty began telling us of her wonderful trip to her brother's home in Abbotsford, B.C. and how, because of an airline strike, she had two extra days of vacation. She remarked how this had been the best home visit she had had with her brother Ted and her sister-in-law Pat for whom Betty felt a deep and genuine affection. Betty loved her family and took enormous pride in her brother's skill at home improvements and gardening. Agatha, as usual, was the quiet listener. She had lost a beloved brother in recent years and could well appreciate Betty's joy in her visit.

The hours passed quickly as we rode through Nova Scotia and into New Brunswick. At about eleven o'clock we approached Fredericton, and, since we hadn't stopped along the way, decided to take an early lunch. Immediately after leaving the city's central core, we stopped at a large gas station, filled up the car, used the washroom facilities, then drove to the back of the station overlooking fields of pine and birch which had already turned to their autumn colors. There was a melancholy tinge to the colours. Quietly, the rain had begun. We ate our lunch in the car. Betty had made tuna fish sandwiches. I had egg salad, and we shared these with Agatha who did not have a lunch. Betty had her thermos of weak tea, I had a flask of strong coffee and Agatha decided she'd buy a bottle of pop.

After our lunch, Agatha volunteered to drive for a few hours, since she knew this part of the road very well. Her brother lived in Edmundston. Betty was relieved because she usually got drowsy after lunch. We changed places in the car. Agatha took the driver's seat, Betty the passenger's and I took the seat behind Betty. Our Pontiac Sunbird took to the road and we were travelling in high spirits, heading for Edmundston, and thence to Houlton, Maine and on to the US 95 highway. We never reached the border.

Teachers at Resurrection-Ascension, Rego Park, NY 1956-1957
From L to R: Sisters Mary Trinita Manning, Helen Eugene McKenna,
John Christopher Verner, Agnes Martha Westwater, Joseph Thomas
Griffin, Gerard Majella Keating, and Mary Cletus Ryan

Pioneers at St. Veronica's, Easter Week 1958. Back row: Sisters Thomas
Gerard D'Entremont, Agnes Martha Westwater, Ann Carmel Harvey

Front row: Sisters Robert Ann Wallace, Marion Catherine Fitzgerald,
Alfred Marie Petralia. Photograph by C. Reg. Vidler, Baie d'Urfee, QC

S. Martha Westwater with Grade 12 class, Our Lady
of Perpetual Help, Vancouver, BC 1966-67

S. Martha Westwater and St. Pat's students, Halifax, 1968

S. Agnes Martha Westwater

Photo of Sister Agnes Martha from Mount Saint
Vincent University Archives 1978-79

S. Martha Westwater receiving honorary degree,
with Dr. Elizabeth Patt-Johnston, President (left) and
Dr. Anna Smol. Mount Saint Vincent University, 1994

S. Martha Westwater, celebrating her Golden Jubilee,
Mount Saint Vincent Motherhouse, June 27, 1999

Sister Martha at the World Trade Center

Sister Agatha Vienneau

Sister Betty Bellefontaine

Namaste Cluster 2014 Martha is front and center

Sister Martha at the March 2017 Meeting in Wellesley

9

Dr. Edward Chalmers Hospital

ABOUT FIVE MINUTES AFTER WE left our luncheon stop, we were on one of the few main highways in New Brunswick that is not divided. Suddenly, out of nowhere it seemed, flashed a white car. I can remember thinking, "What is that maniac doing on our side of the road?" But there was really no time to think, no place to go. To the left was on-coming traffic; to the right a guard rail over a steep precipice. We froze in silent horror as our grey Sunbird Pontiac crashed head first into a white Ford Taurus that was trying to pass a huge lumber truck. The impact was so appallingly violent that I remember the seams of my slacks split from top to bottom. Glass shattered, metal crumpled, but no human voice heard. No terrified shriek, no hysterical screaming, just dead silence. And in that silence that followed the devastating noise, I heard myself groaning, "O God, help us!"; I think that was the closest I came to prayer during the horror of the accident.

Words cannot adequately describe such an experience. Basically, the mind refuses to accept the reality of the situation. It hedges and dodges trying to explain how this event is not real. It can't be happening. It's a dream, a horrible nightmare. As I lifted my head, I saw Betty's little hand on the dashboard and Agatha's head with its crown of little white curls facing the side window and lying on the steering wheel. I recognized the utter stillness of death.

Yet I denied my sisters' deaths. They were only unconscious. How could they be dead and I alive? They would never leave me.

Time had no meaning. How long it was before I became conscious that a crowd of onlookers had gathered, I don't know. I do remember hearing a man's voice declare, "The one in back is still alive. I saw her head move." A young constable from the Royal Canadian Mounted Police managed to reach my hand from the left, back window of the car. He assured me that I was not to worry; that he had seen the accident; it was not our fault; he had called an ambulance, and that it would be at the scene in seven and a half minutes.

Painfully conscious of the seat buckle lodged in my breast and of being unable to move my legs, I managed to give our identification and our destination. I remember the constable calling for the jaws of life and the acrid smell of the blowtorch as preparations were made to extract me out the back window. Weeks later, I recalled feeling guilty for getting out of the car before Betty and Agatha, although I remembered asking the paramedic, "When are my sisters getting out of the car?" He replied that they would be following me to the hospital. They did, but were both declared dead on arrival. I think I lost consciousness once I was wheeled into the emergency room of the Dr. Edward Chalmers Hospital in Fredericton, but not before I gave my brother Bob's phone number. There, no doctors or nurses could have done more to comfort me and repair the multiple fractures I had sustained in both legs, my right wrist and my ribs. Taken singly the injuries were not life threatening but compounded, the situation was critical.

For the next eleven days I was heavily sedated at the Chalmers Hospital, then air-lifted to the Queen Elizabeth II intensive care unit in Halifax. Sisters Maureen and Maria were constant visitors. I remember Maureen's frightened face as she saw me for the first time in the hospital. Her look registered shock and dismay. Maria was much more controlled. She hid her feelings under efficiency. For the long months ahead, when she would visit, usually at night, she would tidy up my room. In the six months of hospitalization, and three more months at the Motherhouse, sisters from Halifax and beyond were there for me. Only one stormy January day, when travelling was dangerous, was I left alone.

It was a long and painful road to recuperation. I have re-lived the tragedy every day for the past eighteen years. The one unanswerable question I ask myself and others is, "Why am I still alive and Betty and Agatha are dead?"

I was still unconscious when Agatha and Betty were buried. Later, after I returned to Halifax and had left the intensive care unit, I remember asking Sister Mary Louise Brink, our congregational leader, if Agatha and Betty were really dead. Had they been buried? She then told me, very gently, how Agatha had been taken to her beloved home in Bathurst, New Brunswick, where she, who did not want any pomp and ceremony for her jubilee, was gloriously sent off to eternity with a bishop and five priests celebrating her funeral Mass. Sister Paule Cantin, who lived with Agatha and was a member of our cluster, gave the homily. It was a magnanimous gesture on Paule's part because originally she and Agatha had been scheduled to drive together to Maine. The day before Paule had come down with the flu, so Agatha travelled to Halifax alone to drive with us. As the body was being carried to the cemetery adjoining the church, children from the school were enjoying a recess period. The air was filled with the joyous sounds of children shrieking at play. Agatha would have loved the sound.

Betty was buried from the Motherhouse in Halifax where she had been ministering as a general councillor on the leadership team. Her recent colleagues from the Religious Studies department at Mount Saint Vincent University were all present and her friend and colleague, Dr. Jacques Goulet, tearfully shrouded her plain grey coffin with the funeral pall, a covering that signifies the baptismal robe, the garment of salvation. For her introductory remarks, Sr. Mary Louise Brink, our congregational leader, remarked on Betty's love for her native city of Halifax and for its people. Bishop Hayes, who gave the homily, commented on Betty's devotion to her call as a Sister of Charity.

Betty and Agatha are buried in different cemeteries in different cities, but they will always be together in our hearts. No two people could have brought us Sisters of Charity closer together than these two women who quietly lived out the charism of charity in totally different ways. In their deaths, we realized anew the glorious call of making God's love visible in our world. Agatha Vienneau and Elizabeth Bellefontaine were good and faithful Sisters of Charity.

Whenever I try to contact Betty and Agatha in prayer, I get the impression that they have moved beyond and want me to let them go. This was more evident with Agatha than it was with Betty. About two weeks before she died, I was taking a long walk with Agatha around Wild Harbor Road in North Falmouth on Cape Cod. We had walked for about an hour and found ourselves a quiet bench looking out over the Atlantic. It was a beautiful September day and Agatha and I exchanged thoughts on our fifty years as Sisters of Charity. I remember telling her that I felt that the best years of my life were over and that I was ready to go home to God. Agatha confided that she wanted no big celebrations for her jubilee, that she too was ready for the final homecoming; there was nothing holding her back. I always go back to that lovely walk when I think of Agatha in her new life. She was ready to go.

Betty was different: Betty had just finished her first year as a member of the leadership team of the Sisters of Charity. When she was elected, Betty gave up her tenured position as a full professor in the Religious Studies Department of Mount Saint Vincent University. However, she discovered new-found capabilities as a councillor. To me, Betty was an open secret. She was open-hearted, fun-loving, the best story-teller (especially of jokes) that I have ever met. And she never repeated a joke or a story. At the same time, Betty was extremely private, soft-spoken, unassuming—a person you could always trust with a confidence. As a councillor on the leadership team, she immediately found her niche. Betty, I feel, is still very interested in what is going on in the congregation. She is easier to reach in prayer than Agatha, but Agatha, in her own way, has looked out for me and in my darkest hour, a thought of Agatha has made me laugh.

What I grieved for most after the accident was the lost goodness of these two sisters. Sometimes we forget that every age has its complement of prophets and holy people—people who make flesh Christ's vision for humanity. We all know of sages and saints who lived long ago and we celebrate their deeds—rightly so. But there are people in our midst who challenge us, who, by their actions and the way they live, help us to hold onto our ideals and to live out their meanings. That is what Betty and Agatha did for me. Without saying a word, but by their actions, I knew they were trying to live the gospel message. That is not to say that they never fell short of their own ideals. But then, we all fall far short of doing what we know is the right thing and we will go into eternity still falling far short of perfection. In the novitiate, I remember reading the life of St. John Berchmans who became a saint in such a short time. In those unrealistic days, I gave myself five years to become a saint. Now, in my old age, I realize that the real challenge to living out the Christian life comes from beginning again after our failures. There is no arrival date for perfection.

That is why the human silence at the time of the accident struck me so forcefully. The secrecy of their hidden lives emanated from their prayer, which was nothing more than the actual, authentic living their faith in Jesus Christ. Prayer formed the foundation of both my sisters' humility.

As they grew in intimacy and knowledge of Christ, neither Betty nor Agatha would take themselves too seriously. They could laugh at their own foibles. From the simplicity of their daily lives, Christ grew within them.

They showed forth the humanity of Christ in their own humanity. The simplicity of their lives can be simply summed up in their doing good and avoiding evil. The first line of the first psalm captures this simplicity: "Happy is the one who refuses the advice of evil."

That word advice carries its own subtle sense of enticement. Evil so often comes disguised as a good: lust disguised as love; greed posing as a legitimate quest for security; covetousness as a feigned need. But Betty and Agatha were deeply conscientious people, ever alert to the subterfuges of others and to the cunning in their own hearts. They both had a basic understanding of themselves and found God in their own humanity. The psalmist tells us quite simply to refuse the advice of evil. Both Agatha and Betty were adamant in their rejection of evil and in their constant seeking after the goodness of God They were very much in touch with themselves, very much aware of their human frailties. Part of the integrity and authenticity of both women developed from their awareness of their own shortcomings and limitations.

That awareness made them understanding of the failures and limitations of others. When one examines their lives, one can see that each found God in the depths of her own human experiences. Both were faithful to prayer and to the demands of the interior life for both solitude and community. But for all their similarities, Agatha and Betty were very different people. I loved them both, but they left me the only survivor of that terrible accident. The question still haunts me: Why was I saved?

In May 1999, I celebrated my Golden Jubilee. I was just learning how to walk again, but I was able to celebrate that joyful day with all my family present. After the celebrations, knowing I had to begin a new life, I returned to Beech Street to begin packing my things for my next mission in Massachusetts.

10

50 Elm Avenue

IT WAS A BEAUTIFUL SEPTEMBER day in 1999 when I left that dear old lady of a city, Halifax, and returned to another old lady of a city, Boston who, by the way, hides her age better. Although Boston is the city of my birth, when I left Canada and returned to the United States, I realized there will always be a part of Canada in me. My maternal grandmother was a Mary Ellen Wallace from Antigonish and my paternal grandmother, Bridget Murphy, came from the outskirts of St. John's, Newfoundland. Between postulate and novitiate training and a long career in education, I had spent forty-five years in Canada. Now I was back home, and I was near my family, who have always been a major source of support and comfort, but I felt rootless.

Upon arriving home again, I moved to a convent in the adjoining city of Quincy. When Sister Esther and her community invited me to join them on Elm Avenue, they could not know the fear, terror and grief that were still a part of my life. They took me in without question, knowing only that I had been involved in a terrible accident. I have always been grateful to them for their kindness.

After three months of acclimatizing myself to my new position as a cripple who still needed two canes to walk, I found myself a position teaching two courses in English Literature and Composition at Massasoit Community College. It was a lifesaving event. During that year, I think I processed the accident as a turning point in my life. I was in my second year of teaching, in 2002, when I remember deciding that I had entered the new millennium as a different person. One day, again in September, as I was walking alone across the courtyard at Massasoit, I became intensely aware of the simple beauty of my surroundings. The courtyard was ablaze with colour, the sun was riding high in a blue sky and I was on my way to class. I remember saying out loud to God or maybe to myself, "I'm happy again." In a paradoxical way, the accident had been a time of grace. In our convent chapel, later that day, I remembered Jesus' words "take up the cross" (Luke 9:24). I thanked the Lord Jesus, perhaps as I never thanked Him before, for his presence in my life. I realized what a blessing that Presence was, along with those other blessings of prayer and community.

Thinking about prayer is like thinking about time. Most of us are not very conscious of time, but to live in time demands our being attentive to the present. Paradoxically, however, most of us live either in the past or in the future. When we are young, it's the future that holds us in thrall. We can hardly wait to begin school, to get into high school, to find a friend, to finish university, to get married, to begin a new job. Even when we seem settled in life, we wish for Friday to come. We spend hours dreaming of Christmas or planning for a vacation.

When we are old, we begin to live in the past, recounting sweet memories, reflecting on our parents' lives, unearthing all we can about our past. Because nostalgia feeds memory with more positive than negative thoughts, it is easy to believe that the past was good to us. We feel safe in the past. But since the accident, I am learning to be more attentive to the present, and the Lord of the Present is the Risen Christ.

We all know that we must inevitably leave time, but we are not very attentive to the glory of eternity—at least I was not.

Indeed, few of us can picture an everlasting life. It remains an impenetrable mystery. The accident helped me live comfortably with that mystery. How we are united with God in eternity is beyond human comprehension, but that I shall be united with my Creator, somehow, sometime, someplace is for me a certainty. That certainty is the ground point of my faith and that faith is nourished by prayer.

I had difficulty in picturing Betty and Agatha in eternity, but I knew that in prayer we contact eternity. Time and eternity are one when we live within. A good two weeks after the accident, while I was still on life support systems, I had my first prayerful encounter with my friends. By this time, I had been airlifted from the Chalmers Hospital in Fredericton, New Brunswick to the Queen Elizabeth II Hospital in Halifax, Nova Scotia. I was still in the intensive care unit, and, though conscious, I was agitated and afraid. My memories (or hallucinations) are of people wailing and of doctors and nurses donning what I suspected were wet suits. I thought of people dying, of bodies being hosed, and I wondered if the intensive care unit was near the morgue. I was terribly frightened.

The ventilator caused me great distress and contributed to my panic. I found it difficult to breathe. In my terror, I prayed to Betty and Agatha to help me not to panic, to help me get rid of the tube in my throat. My two sisters helped: to this day I have no recollection of that tube actually being removed. I simply remember the first few sips of glorious water and how blessed I was to be able to swallow again.

A more personal encounter occurred about three weeks after the accident. Because I needed help in coping with survival guilt, a psychologist counsellor met with me during that initial period of recovery. I could not accept the fact that I was alive and that my two sisters were dead and buried. I did not attend their funerals. I did not say goodbye. They had gone into eternity, and I was still here on earth.

During one of our sessions together, my counsellor urged me to ask Betty and Agatha what they desired for me. That night, when the slough of despondency seemed most acute and when I was afraid to sleep, I prayed to Agatha and Betty and asked them what they would want for me. Betty's answer was gentle and loving: "Do all that you can to get well. Work hard. Do what you are told." Agatha's response was direct and to the point: "Stop bugging me!"

Both answers were so typical. Immediately, I asked Betty to take care of my body and I asked Agatha to take care of my mind. Agatha's response had made me laugh inwardly, and it was the first time I had laughed since the accident. Her response also convinced me that there is an entirely new dimension to life hereafter and that we must be willing to let our loved ones be free to enjoy their new life.

Some people might discount such an incident as simply prayer. But what I've learned at this point in my life is that deep within us all there is a private resting place, the one that St. Teresa of Avila called an interior castle; a secret garden where we contact that Divine Voice with whom we constantly communicate, trying to discover God's will for us. That is why the mystery of the Annunciation holds such meaning for prayer. At the most unexpected times, God enters our lives. When the angel appeared to Mary, she was afraid. The fear I felt in the aftermath of the accident was intensely real. I, who most times whined about being left behind, paradoxically feared my present precarious hold on life. In the fear and chaos of illness, my only resort was prayer—prayer in which I merely existed. Time ceases to be in the inner sanctuary of prayer. There are no words, no formulae, no mental activity of any kind. Those who have died have entered into the timelessness of eternity and only in prayer could I discover such timelessness.

But time does not become holy, does not become prayer, until we have learned to discover the mystery of God in human experience, to find God's will in which alone is our peace. I did not understand the meaning of my losses—the loss of two dear sisters and friends, of control over my own body, of my independence. Yet deep within these losses, I entered into the eternal now of prayer.

Though I move with leaden feet. Light itself is not
   so fleet;
And before you know me gone
Eternity and I are one.

These lines are from "Time," by William Dean Howells. Only in prayer could I enter into the timelessness of eternity, and that is how I could reach Betty and Agatha.

It was not that I hadn't prayed or tried to "let go" of worldly matters before the accident. One of the greatest graces of my life, as I have already mentioned, was the long retreat of thirty days that I made after I completed my doctoral studies. At that point, I truly believed I had become rooted in Christ. Now I knew that my roots were not deep enough. I also thought I knew the significance of praying in the aridity of the empty tomb, but I still had so much to learn. It was only in the months of recovery that I discovered that often I had forced myself to try to recapture the human Christ in His words, His teachings, the events of His life. But the Christ of the present is the Risen Christ, no longer in the tomb. He is in and with the Creator God and the Holy Spirit. Prayer had now become discovering myself in the Godhead.

Not that the humanity of Christ was forgotten—impossible! The humanity and divinity of Christ are inseparable. That is why the Eucharist and devotions that focus on the humanity of Christ, such as the rosary, are incomparable links to prayer. What I write on prayer in these pages is not specifically from Ignatius Loyola, Garigou Lagrange, Karl Rabner or Thomas Merton, although being brought up in the spiritual life on these teachers, I suspect there is a bit of all of them here. Like the earthly wife of Bath, I take experience as my authority. And, like Dame Alisoun and the majority of human beings, deep within my being there is an unquenchable quest for intimacy. Very early in life that desire surfaced, and very early in my spiritual life, I had to learn that intimacy with God is not the same thing as intimacy with another human being, although such intimacy does not necessarily preclude it. Sometimes, I think we expect spiritual intimacy to correspond to sensual intimacy. What emptiness results from that misunderstanding!

To pray or to seek intimacy with God is to encounter nothingness, and yet to know nothingness is to possess everything. It is like entering a labyrinth, the way of the pilgrim. There is only one path that leads to the centre of the labyrinth of our being, where we can discover our centredness in God. However, when we walk a labyrinth, we seem at times to be moving away from the centre. Sometimes we can't be sure where the centre is and oftentimes, just when we think we are getting far away, lo there we are, right in the centre of the All Holy.

During the third week of recovery, when I was in a ward with three other very sick people, a friend brought me a tape of Cardinal Bernardin's life. I could not read, nor hold a book; formal morning and night prayers were impossible, but I could listen to a tape. I think I really began to pray when I heard Cardinal Bernardin quote St. Paul: "Christ Jesus emptied himself taking the form of a servant" (Phil. 2:6). That one phrase, "emptied himself" become my lifeline. I discovered meaning in the emptying process which the aftermath of the accident entailed. In the long tedious months ahead, alone in my hospital room trying to pray, I simply let myself flow with the emptying. I'd find myself staring out the window watching the pigeons on the hospital roof. Peacefully gazing at the birds, watching their frenzied flights and landings, saying nothing, thinking nothing, just being still, watching without words, content to be in harmony with my world as it was. This was my prayer.

Sometimes I wondered whether the experience was real or imagined prayer. I really can never be certain about what constitutes true prayer. However, this I know—I feel the presence of God when I least expect it. I cannot will or manipulate it in any way. The Godhead is far, far beyond my petty attempts to capture It. Fleeting are these moments when we sense the peace of God's presence; but in silently watching the birds, I entered into timelessness and felt the power of God's love when I least expected it. I can't explain it further. I know my faith in God whose love was made visible in his care of the birds saved me from despair.

Not that I did not worry about my situation! My legs had been broken severely in several places. There was the possibility that I might never walk again. My body seemed not my own. In its weakness and pain it became a harsh tormentor and I desired to escape from it. The question I asked myself constantly was: Why was I saved and my two companions killed? Of course, there was no answer. Neither was there any answer to those other riddles: Why did I take my car when it had no airbags? Why didn't I stay in the front seat beside Agatha and let Betty remain in the back of the car? Hour by hour, day after day, the questions re-surfaced relentlessly and the answers were hopelessly elusive.

I wonder how the three sisters at Elm Avenue were ever able to cope with me. I was still recuperating, more mentally than physically. I always recalled the first meeting I had with a woman psychologist after the accident. I don't remember her name but on her first visit, out of the blue, she asked me very directly: "Would you rather be alive or dead?" I did not answer.

She asked again, "Would you rather live or die?" Her expression indicated that she did not expect to have the answer next week. She wanted it then and there.

Haltingly, even reluctantly, almost sulkily, I stammered, "Well, I am alive, am I not? That's the fact of the matter."

"So," she continued, "would you rather be alive or dead?"

I had to answer her question: "I want to live." It was a simple reply, but it was enormously critical because I had to make a conscious decision to accept the burden of life—painful as that life had become. My psychologist made me articulate my decision to accept life over death, to put some order into the chaos of the crash. If order follows life, then a good life results when we accept the order life imposes.

But it was my faith in a God, who willed that I survive while my two companions finished their journeys, that prompted the reply, "I choose life." My faith saved me. During the next twelve months I would find meaning in the humdrum reality of pain and recovery, of endless physical humiliations, of boring, boring therapy sessions. Faith and time are inextricably twinned because in prayer we exercise faith and only by faith can we enter into prayer. How often do we go to prayer like the father of the son in Mark's gospel who pleaded with the Lord, "If you are able to do anything, have pity on us and help us"(Mark 9:14–29). And Jesus replied with uncharacteristic forcefulness and even with a trace of indignation, "If you are able!—All things are possible for the one who believes." The father's response has become the unspoken *cri de coeur* of every Christian, "I believe; help my unbelief." Our greatest obstacle to prayer is our lack of faith, but it is precisely when we find it difficult to believe that we must pray the longest.

The central article of faith in Christianity is the Resurrection. "If Christ be not risen from the dead, then is our religion vain," warns St. Paul in his first letter to the Corinthians (I Cor. 15:18). If the dead do not rise, neither has Christ been raised and we all are deluded.

Paul unveiled the heart of the matter. The greatest obstacle to prayer is unbelief. If we really examine our lives, how few of us reflect on eternity. Few of us could say with the poet Vaughan:

> I saw Eternity the other night
> Like a great ring of pure and endless light.
> All calm, as it was bright,
> And round beneath it, Time in hours, days, years,
> Driven by the spheres
> Like a vast shadow mov'd; in which the world
> And all her train were hurled.

> "The World." Silex Scintillans.

Betty and Agatha had entered into that "great ring of pure and endless light." Agatha, I suspect, would not want to enter any further into our earthly life. Betty, I think, would like to drop in on our world now and again. But they have gone into that realm of timelessness and they wanted me to let them go. Prayer showed me God's will for me in the eternal present. In God, yesterday, today and forever are one.

I shall always be grateful to Sister Esther for inviting me, broken in body, to St. Elizabeth Seton Convent on Elm Avenue, Quincy. I missed Canada; I who prayed that I would be nearer home so I could visit my mother was now home, but my mother had gone. I had two brothers and a loving sister in the Boston area, and another brother and sister in Virginia. We had always been a very close and loving family, but now I had to begin a new life in community.

I was back in a convent with a chapel and the Blessed Sacrament. This was indeed a blessing for me. I lived with two other remarkable women: Sister Mary Corona and her biological sister, Sister Rita MacDonald. It was a busy house as all three were actively engaged in ministry. At ninety, dear Sister Corona led two choirs, two evening practices and three masses on Sunday. Sister Rita had a Young Mothers group and Esther, a liturgist and a stalwart choir member, was working to establish the only Catholic high school for girls in the Boston area.

Perhaps the greatest aid to my recovery and living a full life came from my family—especially from the new generation of Westwaters. My nephew, Robert Leo Westwater II had married Julie Howley, and Bob and Julie made their home mine. Their four children were Patrick, four years old; Maeve, two; and Maureen, an infant. Robert Leo was born in 2000, so I have known him all his life. I looked forward to playing with the children more than socializing with the adults. These four children saved me from depression.

It must have been difficult for my religious sisters and my family, especially Joanne and Bob, because at this period I was finding it difficult to settle in and find community. For all their kindnesses, I felt different from the other members of the small community of four, three of whom had lived together for so many years. Aims and objectives had already been established, but I felt I was not a part of their making. However, two new activities saved me: my teaching at Massasoit and Casino nights on Friday.

At the college, five of us uniquely different adjunct professors, with ages ranging from early thirties to late seventies, shared a windowless office. The unusual differences among us made for an equally unusual, congenial group. Between classes we shared stimulating conversations, offering widely different perspectives, on subjects ranging from views on teaching Comp I to the much broader issues of educational philosophy, religion, science and politics. I found myself in a less cerebrally challenging environment, but in a more stimulating metaphysical one. Perhaps it was the events of September 11, 2001 that cemented the vibrant bonding among us.

We were in our over-stuffed, windowless office when the planes struck the towers. We had no television, but already we knew that it was a terrorist attack. We were advised to remain in place until a safe evacuation could be executed. I remember a comment one of my colleagues made while we were waiting. She said, with more than a touch of anger, "The sooner we get rid of every temple, church and mosque, the safer we'll be." I was struck dumb by that statement. Then a young Jewish gentleman, still working on his dissertation, remarked that it was not religion but extremism in religion that was the problem. Mary, who was to become a close friend, said that, as a Christian, she felt the problem was that we had forgotten the chief tenet of Christianity—love of God and love of neighbour. Another woman, the wittiest among us, said that the most moderate religion, and the least bent towards extremism, was the United Universalist Church, which embraces all religions and satisfies our deepest need for spirituality and community. At that time, I had not told my confreres that I was a Sister of Charity, but I felt I had to contribute to the conversation which was respectful, earnest and honest. I agreed with Mary's view on Christianity and simply added that I was a Sister of Charity dedicated, quite simply, to making love visible in the world.

In that dingy, crowded office, I have never felt more confident of my call to give joyful witness to love and never have I felt such a love for all God's people. It was not a love limited to the four other teachers in the room, but they seemed to represent a microcosm of all humanity. I was overwhelmed with love for the people in the high-jacked plane who faced a horrible death, to the people in the towers who were incinerated, to the first responders who set up triage stations, to the firemen who worked heroically to save the people in the towers and who died for them. Since the events of 9/11, the world has changed. Worse than the despondency following the Vietnam War was the fear and terror incited by suicide bombers who lost respect for their own lives and for the lives of thousands of others.

Work is the antidote to despair and the everyday pursuits of making a living helped people accept the reality of the present. With unusual energy, ordinary life resumed and the sublime endeavour to get on with life, to find enjoyment in the simple game of life subdued the grief and terror of the events of 9/11.

Almost as disastrous as the events of 9/11 was the sexual abuse scandal in the Archdiocese of Boston, which broke in the Boston Globe in 2002. What most angered me about this heartbreaking news was that on the Saturday when the Globe published the names of the priests who had abused children, nothing was mentioned from the pulpit about these devastating revelations. No words of comfort or apology to the victims of abuse; no solace or consolation to assuage the grief of devoted Catholics who had to bear the shame of the despicable actions on the part of their priests. It was a terrible blow to the credibility of the church and to the integrity of its hierarchy. Cardinal Bernard Law bore most of the blame for the cover-up; he allowed the transferring of priests from parish to parish even though accusations had been brought to his attention. In subsequent explanations for his conduct, Law maintained that the Archdiocese did not have the expertise to deal with pedophilia.

The scandal made me realize how little education we received in the novitiate in sexual matters. Sexual sins were always mortal. Younger sisters in formation had received some instruction and I think they were more tolerant of priestly failures. Nothing toppled priests from their lofty pedestals more than the abuse scandal in Boston, which led to investigations in all dioceses in the United States and in some dioceses in Europe.

Quite preposterously during these tumultuous days, the activity that helped me feel closer to my community was instigating a Casino Night at 50 Elm Avenue. My sister Joanne, a Good Shepherd sister, felt more at home at Elm Avenue than I did. She suggested playing cards on Friday nights. Knowing the Boston sisters better than I did, she invited five mutual friends and sisters to cards. We would each take a night to act as hostess, a commitment that involved preparing a meal, which was followed by a game of Penny Rummy. I began enjoying being a hostess, planning the evening, preparing a meal, making people comfortable and happy.

The game is 10 percent luck, 10 percent concentration and 80 percent hilarity. Paradoxically, the hilarity became a point of contention for the sisters with whom I lived. I took their disapproval personally and felt angry. In examining my anger, however, I discovered how dependent I had become on the approval of others. This was a transformative moment. I felt a new surge of independence, a way of coping with disapprobation.

There was a strange mixture of petulance and joy at the time, but I realized that I had come of age and no longer had to rely on the approval of others. My year at 50 Elm Avenue was a bridge year. I passed from desiring, actually needing, the approval of others to becoming more comfortable with the person I was or had become. I needed a new space and I began looking for another community.

11

17 Hutchinson Street

In June of 2001, I moved to the Lower Mills section of Dorchester. I was living in a two-family, white, vinyl-shingled house originally intended for five sisters, but now sheltering a quiet community of three: Kathleen, Peg and me. As different as we were, we were united in one significant matter. We all loved privacy and at 17 Hutchinson Street, we had it.

The house boasted a front and back porch. When I moved in, the front porch hosted a robin's nest in its eves, and the back porch had a clothes line. That was the big attraction for me; I could hang out wet clothes to dry in the sun. The house was surrounded by trees and the back yard had a little garden in which I could putter—another soothing attraction.

It was now more than thirty years since the Chapter of Renewal in 1968 and life was very different. For the most part, prayer was private. I was still teaching at Massasoit Community College, and left very early in the morning, whereas the other two sisters left home later, after the early morning traffic had abated. I was the oldest at seventy-two; the others were over the retirement age, but still active. Volunteering was the new ministry. Kathleen volunteered at our retirement home in Wellesley and Peg had a parish ministry.

When I say we took our prayers privately, in no way do I want to intimate that we did not pray. Both sisters I lived with were deeply spiritual women and we informally shared spiritual insights. But the life we lived in common was driving prayer more deeply within; prayer was more personal than communal. We were far more honest with one another; we were able to express individual needs. For example, in the beginning we did try taking turns to prepare the nightly meal, but it became too difficult as time went on. As one sister stated, Route 128 was horrendously traffic logged. She volunteered in a nursing home and travelled this route twice daily and so began taking her main meal at her place of ministry. We ended up preparing our meals privately. All three of us were now in our late sixties and early seventies, and were freed from the duty of cooking for others. I enjoyed the freedom of cooking for myself, of having what I wanted, when I wanted it. Was I becoming more self-centred?

When the 1968 chapter advocated respect for the individual sister, it was the word "individual" that was considered most significant. The old style community, when thirty of us would pray together, walk to church together, take meals together, recreate together, was long gone. Certainly I prized the new freedom, although I did question whether I was enjoying it too much. Was I becoming too individualistic? Did my good come before the good of the community? I began to realize that the community is as good as the individual sister. As different as we three sisters were in temperament, values and interpretation of the gospel, I knew that each of my sisters was following Christ as her conscience directed. Each one was committed to make the love of God visible in today's world in her own distinctive manner. Although we did not hold formal meetings to discuss community affairs, we did discuss community and congregational matters. And I knew that prayer was an essential part of my sisters' lives.

The world of the Sisters of Charity had changed and, thank God, we had changed with it. The well-established schools, with many sections of the same grade, which required twenty to thirty sister teachers were now run mostly by seculars. At our peak in the 1950s, we numbered nearly 1,700 sisters; in 2006, that number was about 700. We had to face the fact that no new members had entered religious life in the past thirty years. As an organized religious group, we Sisters of Charity were dying.

Paradoxically, we had more life. We were looking beyond the four walls of the classroom, of the hospital, of the office. We were looking at worldwide challenges: the melting of the ice cap, the genocides in Africa, the wars that begot widespread displacements. Personally, at this time, I was genuinely moved by the situation in the Sudan, a tragic victim of colonialism.

Sudan achieved independence from British administration in 1956, but with several military coups, two civil wars and a series of severe famines, the country was both economically and politically destabilized. Sudan contains two distinct cultures: black African and Arabic. The black African population is ethnically diverse and concentrated mainly in the south; Arabic-speaking Muslims belong to several ethnic groups and live mainly in the northern and central parts of the country.

Sudan's north-south war is a tale of unfathomable horror: of genocide, of slave selling, of Islamic-Christian tensions, of pastoralist and agriculturist scuffles, of northern militia killings, of women being raped and children turned into soldiers, of half a million people being displaced. Sudanese atrocities were highlighted when international attention centred on human rights violations in Darfur. It was at this point that I felt moved to help with the ministry in South Sudan.

I had heard of a Teachers College run by *Solidarity with Southern Sudan*, and I volunteered to teach English there. Looking back, I recognize pride in my offer, but I felt I could do some good teaching English to South Sudanese teachers. I wrote a letter explaining my qualifications (I'm certain I embellished them), but my application for a teaching position was rejected. I must admit that letter containing the news was the longest, most laudatory rejection letter I have ever received.

Instead of offering me a position as a teacher, *Solidarity* asked me if I would be willing to write a newsletter for them. The idea excited me. In a country where 92% of the people lived below the poverty line, where adult illiteracy had been estimated at a staggering 85%, where only 25% of the children were enrolled in primary school, where only 2.3% completed primary education and where, in many places, schooling took place under a tree because only 10% of the children attended school with formal classrooms, *Solidarity* was making a difference. In ten years, over 140 religious congregations had contributed to its growth. *Solidarity*'s staff consisted of twenty-three sisters, brothers and priests from thirteen different congregations and fourteen nationalities. By 2010, two teacher training campuses for pre-service instruction had been prepared in Malakai and in Yambio. Over 600 primary school teachers had received in-service training to enhance teaching competence. The country still needed tens of thousands more teachers, but *Solidarity*, at that time, was the largest provider of teacher training in the country. I'm happy to relate that our own Sister Yvonne Pothier joined the teaching team at Solidarity and gave two years of her life to its service.

With regard to health education, the extensive renovations at the *Catholic Health Training Institute* in Wau had been completed. In addition to the improved facilities, an internationally certified Registered Nursing program had been established. I took pride in trumpeting these successes in the newsletter.

Sadly, I had to give up the newsletter when a new director wanted less text and more pictures. I did not have the necessary technical expertise, and I was too old to learn. However, I was able to report on the crucial referendum of January 9, 2011, when the people of Southern Sudan voted overwhelmingly to secede, and to become South Sudan. Unfortunately, as I write now, in 2016, after

the glorious promises of new prosperity and independence, South
Sudan is again at war with the North.

I cited this involvement with South Sudan to illustrate how
our world had broadened. As I write, another one of our sisters,
Jolaine States, a psychologist, is serving the needs of the children in
Kenya. That broadening sense of place was matched by our different
attitudes to time as well.

As a congregation, we were thinking of that time when the last
Sister of Charity would have died. How would we insure our legacy?
We began thinking and talking about establishing a foundation that
would continue our mission to give joyful witness to God's love by
serving those in need. Rooted in that mission, the foundation would
strive to right in great ways or small, the injustices we saw around us.
Establishing such a foundation would require money—more than
I could imagine. It would demand more letting go, more selling of
property. The Motherhouse had already been demolished and we
were in the process of selling the land. Now we began to sell houses
that we were unable to maintain. Our home on Hutchinson Street
was scheduled for the real estate market.

My first reaction to the news that our house would be sold was
disbelief and anger. I had to make a choice between going to our
retirement home or finding an apartment. It was a very difficult
choice. I wanted to continue teaching at Massasoit, but I did not
want to give up community or the community-owned car needed for
transportation to work. My two companions had chosen to move to
individual, one-bedroom apartments in a huge complex consisting
of two very large buildings. I looked only at the outside of the
buildings, which seemed to me like impressive hotels. Even though
the building overlooked beautiful Dorchester Bay, I made up my
mind to find another smaller apartment in a less imposing setting.

12

65 Elmwood Drive

ALTHOUGH I CONSIDERED MYSELF INDEPENDENT and able to cope with sudden change, I had no idea what was involved in getting a house ready for the realtor. I never knew the amount of work demanded. Thank God, Peg, as bursar, had kept the house in excellent repair and that Kathleen had already closed one house and was somewhat of an expert in house-moving; she was a quiet, easy-going, hard-working professional. We decided that each would take the floor where we had our bedrooms and personal belongings. Peg took the attic and the adjoining storeroom; Kay took the first floor, and I the second. We would take whatever furniture we needed for our apartments and give any remaining furniture to charities like Goodwill or My Brothers' Keeper.

Peg had already moved, so the top floor was cleared. Kay and I worked together in packing dishes, furniture, linens etc. If I thought I had rid myself of "stuff" when I left Halifax, I was grossly mistaken! All the transcriptions of the Bagehot diaries, all lecture notes for Victorian Prose and Poetry, all notes on texts for Children's Literature, Freshman Composition and Literature—it all went to trash. I was sad to see it go.

All the while, in the midst of this Mother of all Cleanups, I had to find an apartment. My sister, Joanne, was most helpful. She looked at several for me and encouraged me to find a two-bedroom unit. However, it was a family connection and dear friend who found me a one-bedroom apartment on a secluded street in a quiet neighbourhood. I would move into 65 Elmwood Park, and I would enjoy real solitude for the first time in my life.

I was excited about the move. My apartment was on the first floor. It had a comfortably open living room with a small dining area next to the kitchen, and a large bedroom easily accommodating a bookcase and computer. Best of all, there were two large closets. What gave me most pleasure, however, was a tiny enclosed balcony. I had moved in during the summer, so I had flowering plants and geraniums that I had taken from Hutchinson Street. For prayer I had flowers and sky. What more did I need? But how different life had become from those early days in the congregation! Sitting on the balcony I reflected on those changes. I was wearing casual, light summer clothes and was relieved that I did not have the heavy woollen habit of yesteryear. I never heard a bell summoning me from sleep or to go to Mass, meals or prayer. Yet I still went to daily Mass, prayed even more, because I had more time, made my own meals and ate when I wanted. I enjoyed my freedom. There was one freedom I would gladly relinquish and that was dealing with money. I could rarely get the monthly financial report to balance. How I wished I had taken at least one business course!

During my second year at Elmwood Drive I took a year-long course in spiritual direction. I had reached my eightieth year and had never had a spiritual director; what is more, I never felt the need of one. I signed up for the course, not so much to direct others (I recognized my own inadequacy), but because I wanted to deepen my own prayer life, to prepare for my seeing the Face of God.

We were a group of twelve very diverse individuals: an Anglican Pastor, a divorced mother, a gay businessman, housewives, professionals and two religious. But what we all had in common was the experience of God in prayer. We met once a week for nine months. We studied Ignatian spirituality, but most of all we prayed and shared encounters with the transcendent—simple encounters where the very ordinary became extraordinary. I remember one experience I had that struck me forcibly. Joanne had given me several unused Dunkin Donuts gift cards. She never bought her morning coffee there, but she knew I liked DD coffee, but was too cheap to buy it. One evening, while driving home from a visit with Joanne, and talking simply to the Lord, I was struck with the idea of redeeming all those gift cards for bags of the famous coffee, which I then could brew myself. It was a simple, obvious idea, but, like so many other ideas that come in prayer, I took an electric kind of joy in the idea. It was evening at a time when there would be few customers. I went into the shop, asked if I might redeem my cards for bags of coffee and exited the shop with six pounds of my highly-prized Dunkin Donuts coffee. Nothing could convince me that this wasn't a loving, direct gift from the God of Love and Mystery.

Another gift from the program was learning to pay closer attention to dreams. One dream, rather a nightmare, was a recurring experience of being tied to a green, slimy, algae-covered pole holding up a long wharf. I was submerged in water and struggling. I usually woke up, terrified. Reflecting on that dream, I came to realize that, after the accident, my subconscious had retained the experience of being strapped on a pallet, and carried through the dark night sky from the New Brunswick to the Halifax hospital after the accident. The nightmare lost its power.

The spiritual direction program was a great blessing, chiefly because the main retreat house was located in Cohasset overlooking the mighty Atlantic. The house itself, an old Victorian mansion, sat atop a rock-fortressed hill, and, if you were limber enough, you could scramble down those rocks and kiss the ocean, a perfect symbol of infinity. Along with other losses, this lovely old house and the magnificent surrounding property, reluctantly, will be handed over to a realtor.

But the loss of a house is nothing compared to the loss of the parents and siblings with whom you once shared a house. My father bought the house at 6 St. Margaret Street before the Great Depression of 1929, the year I was born. I had just turned six when my father died in 1935. Agnes, my oldest sister died at twenty-one before I entered religious life. She had finished teachers college and had been granted a teaching position in the Boston Public Schools. After two or three days of teaching, she sickened, and was found to have a streptococcus infection. This was before the days of penicillin and she died four months later, January 17, 1943. Her death was a heartbreak for all of us, but our grief was miniscule in comparison with the grief my mother experienced. My darling mother died on July 30, 1963. She was the greatest loss of my life. Agnes was the greatest spiritual influence in my life, but my mother was my greatest love and inspiration.

There followed almost forty years before my brother Donald died at eighty-two. My most cherished memory of Donald is his surprise visit the day I had to defend my Ph.D. dissertation. He took a plane from Boston and met me as I emerged from the exam room. It was such an overwhelming expression of family love, I cried. Donald was the most secretive of us all. Only at his wake did we realize that in World War II he was the recipient of the Bronze Star and the Combat Infantry Badge. He was among those who closed down the concentration camps after the war ended. He never spoke of his experiences. Instead, he took full advantage of the G.I. Bill of Rights went to college, received his law degree and practiced criminal law in Boston.

My sister Evelyn died on December 21, 2006, just six months after her husband John E. Doyle. After my mother died, Evelyn and John made their home mine. I was closest to Evelyn, beautiful, honest, Evelyn. She was a deep thinker and an avid golfer. I think it was her love of life that I most appreciated, and it took me a long time to grieve after her death.

My brother Joseph died two years later on December 29, 2008. Enlisting in the Coast Guard at seventeen, he served on the *USS Storis*, on convoy patrol in the North Atlantic during World War II. A family man first and foremost, Joe gave up his research for his doctorate in economics because with five young children, he simply did not have time for study. He was tremendously proud of his wife, his son and his four daughters.

The last to leave me was my sister Joanne, a Good Shepherd Sister who had an inspiring love of the poor. She founded the Maria Droste Services in Quincy, Massachusetts, where she lived out the spirit of the Good Shepherd. Joanne had a deep compassion for the poor, the oppressed, the rejected. She lived among the poor in a one-bedroom apartment, and I shall never forget how loving she was towards the mentally challenged in her building. Once when I was writing some bills for her, the telephone rang and she forgot I was there and concentrated on the problems of one of her clients. She died March 8, 2015, of a massive heart attack in my car as I was about to drive her to Mass and a jubilee luncheon. Having to face living in a retirement home, she beat the system. Joanne's death caused me deep, deep pain.

Now there is only my younger brother Robert Leo and his family who are my family now, and how blessed I am to have this Howley-Westwater union. I am also blessed in having the Westwater-Doyle connection. Linda Holland Doyle calls me every Monday morning to keep me informed of Doyle family matters. I'll not grieve for Evelyn while I have generous, loving Linda. I also have eleven faithful nieces and nephews, twenty-four grand nieces and nephews and seven great-grand nieces and nephews. The family is still increasing!

13

125 Oakland Street

I AM WRITING THIS SHORT memoir after completing two years in our retirement house. When did I decide to come to Marillac Residence? It happened on a sunny Saturday morning in May when Sister Mary Sweeney and I decided to view the lilacs in the Arnold Arboretum. As we arrived, I stepped out of the car and had a dizzy spell—as simple as that. I sent Mary along to enjoy the lilacs and I found the nearest bench, sat down, watched young parents playing with their children and decided that it was time for me face reality: I was old. What if this dizzy spell happened when I was driving? What if it's a precursor to something more serious? It was time for me to move. What a blessing that I had another home to welcome me in my old age!

So here I am. As in most changes in moving to a new house, there are advantages and disadvantages, losses and gains. Although the disadvantages and losses were genuine, they were far, far outweighed by the advantages and gains. Perhaps the most obvious loss was that of independence. I no longer had my own apartment, a bank account or the autonomy that comes from a monthly direct deposit of my pension. On the other hand, I didn't have the monthly headache of balancing my cheque book or of justifying expenses in the monthly account for the finance office in Halifax. Then there was the giving up of the car that never belonged to me anyway; the car was purchased in the name of the Sisters of Charity. Strictly speaking, I had only the use of it; however, living alone, I had *exclusive* use of it.

The one extraordinary gain of moving to Marillac, our retirement house, was the opportunity of sharing life with sixty-two good, faithful religious women. I had taken living with *good* people very much for granted. In his Letter to the Philippians, St. Paul wrote: "Make my joy complete by your unanimity, possessing the one love, united in spirit and ideals" (Phil. 2:2). We sisters at Marillac are united in spirit and ideals, even though, at least for myself, I know I have not yet achieved that ideal of "think[ing] others as superior to themselves, each looking to others' interests rather than her own."(Phil. 2:2–4, 14–16). We are also supposed to "act without grumbling," but some of us still do—grumble that is—especially about meals.

Overall, I live with very good people who have consecrated their lives for the service of others. They manifest that goodness in completely different ways. Some serve the sick and infirm in our Elizabeth Seton Residence, a long-term rehabilitation and retirement home; some teach in our *One Small Step Program* designed to help our employees, who are mostly immigrants, learn English. Most, with faith-filled confidence, strive cheerfully with the aches, pains and discomforts of the aging process. After eighty, it's downhill all the way!

In our chapel, on either side of a magnificent, dominating crucifix, there are two green banners—one depicts the three intertwining circles symbolizing the Holy Trinity, and the other, a cross. It is the Trinitarian symbol which is significant for me because it helps me reconcile the relationship between God, the All Good, me and the sisters with whom I live. The vows bind us in those intertwining circle. Through chastity, we choose to seek the Love of God in our love for all people; through poverty, we give any wealth we have for service to our fellow creatures; through obedience, we pledge to be involved with those in leadership in seeking how to effect the greater good for all in the congregation and in our world. The intertwining circles represent the relationships between God, Me and Others. To maintain the union of the three separate rings, I must immerse myself in this holy trinity and realize that at some point one ring must bend to the other parts. This chapel banner illustrates life in Marillac in this still-changing era.

The banners change from season to season. Change is always a constant in our lives and there have been changes, immense changes for us old timers.

Take for example our thinking about God's creation of the world, Christ's incarnation in that world and our involvement with all of creation. In *The New Cosmology and Christian Faith*, Sister Donna Geernaert helped us understand the inter-relatedness of God, the works of creation and human beings. She explains how cosmologies "are important because they offer a world view saying who we humans are in relation to God, the world, and one another."[15] This relationship between God, the cosmos and us humans offers another concept of the intertwining circles. Our thinking has moved beyond the chapel to the world, although the words of the psalmist are as applicable now in 2016 CE as they were in 2016 BCE: "I have looked on thee in thy sanctuary,/ beholding thy power and thy glory" (Psalm 63). Indeed, I still find God's Presence in the Blessed Sacrament reserved in the tabernacle, but I also find it sitting on a bench on the brow of a Wellesley hill overlooking a lovely copse of bushes and trees where thousands of birds find sanctuary, squirrels browse for food and even a deer will take her fawn to see the wonders of this brave new world. The intertwining circles of the banner relate to the belief that God is unity in trinity. As Sister Donna explains, "it is mutual interrelatedness that maintains the identity and difference of Persons in this Three-in-One God. In brief God's To Be is to Be In Relationship."[16] How life-giving is this new teaching on the relationship between God, the world and the self.

When first we entered religious life, we were taught that we should be dead to the world; we were even given a new name and a new identity. I was Sister Agnes Martha and we never used our surname. There were no radios, TVs, newspapers or cars. (How extraordinary that the automobile has come to signify our independence!) In those early days, most reading, outside educational material, was spiritually orientated. Silence pervaded the house except at recreation, which was taken in common in the community room. Most meals were taken in silence.

How different is life now. Strangely, however, at Marillac, with the exception of the entrance foyer, dining room and administrative offices on the ground floor, silence, or better still, a gentle quietness still pervades the house. The stillness emanates from the chapel where each morning we meet the Lord and each other for the celebration of the Eucharist. All are invited to this banquet. It is the one act of the day in which we all participate—even the sick and bed-ridden join us by means of television.

However, there are other small changes that have immense significance. For the first time, a sister does not lead us. We have an earnest cheerful, energetic caregiver who loves us and who realizes the importance of God in our lives. There are other little changes. No longer do we greet each other with "Praise be to Jesus," as we did in long-ago days. Now we greet each other with a wave or a simple "Hi!" We have no rule of silence, but stillness still reigns in our long, cheerful, corridors. Retirement is very different for us three congregations—Sisters the of Charity, the Religious of Jesus and Mary, and the Marist Sisters—all aging together, but the triad of relationships still holds: God, our vows and our dealings with one another. Each has her own gifts; no one has all of them, but there are enough gifts here to effect much good. There is a love energy in the house that gives me comfort.

Retirement is easy if we allow ourselves to become involved in all the activities of the house, if we continue to be of service to others whether that means teaching English to employees, visiting the sick at Elizabeth Seton Residence, making lunches for the homeless at holiday times, giving to the various charitable works of the sisters, and then, perhaps the most important work—praying for the needs of the world. The most important rule for a happy life in retirement is to become involved.

In addition to teaching, I have been writing the obituaries of the sisters who die here in the United States. I think that in reflecting on the lives of these sisters I have come to discover that prayer united them with their God and contributed to their genuine holiness. So much is revealed in the sharing that is done at the Wake Service before burial. Yes, the sisters' accomplishments are recognized, but more significant are the joy and service that they contributed to community living. On the other hand, there are those who seemingly had few accomplishments; their lives were marked by suffering, spiritual and physical; yet, there is that element of prayer, their answering to the call of intimacy with God that marks these sisters' lives. Writing these obituaries has been a great grace for me.

So, here I am beginning my third year at Marillac, looking back on a long, happy life as a Sister of Charity. Whenever the old question arises, "Why have I lived and Agatha and Betty died?" (and it does come up often, but certainly not as often as it did in the three years following the accident), I think it might be to tell this story, which is really a conclusion to that story I began over fifty years ago in *Nothing on Earth*. The momentous changes following the Vatican II Council disrupted what I considered a peaceful, happy life. I was reluctant to make those changes but now realize that those changes have deepened my spiritual life. The essence of religious life has remained the same. The consecrated woman religious seeks a living relationship with the Resurrected Christ, by observing the evangelical counsels of poverty, chastity and obedience for the service of her neighbour. It is this living relationship to the Resurrected Christ that must be emphasized.

After the Resurrection, Jesus took different forms. It seems that in most cases, He was at first not recognized. Mary thought He was the gardener; the Emmaus men thought he was merely one of the pilgrims who didn't know what was going on at the Passover celebration; Thomas thought He was a ghost and would not believe until he intimately felt the Christ. Christ meets us in our time and place. We just need eyes to see.

It took me many years to see the living Christ in the way we now live religious life. It's a new age and I am still a little attached to the old. However, more will be demanded of the New Age Christians who choose to leave all for love of God and service to their neighbour. The new religious will need more courage to face failure in herself and others; more discipline not to make prayer subservient to service; more trust in God, Who is increasingly ignored or considered irrelevant, and perhaps most importantly, the new religious will need a more measureless, self-giving love. I believe that those coming of age in the Catholic Church at this time in our history have that courage, discipline, trust and love.

During the past month, September 2016, three religious women working with the poor were robbed and murdered. Two sisters, one a Franciscan and the other a Sister of Charity of Nazareth were nurse practitioners in a medical clinic in Mississippi; the third sister was a Religious of Jesus and Mary who ran a prosthetic clinic in Haiti. All three were women who consecrated their lives to the service of God's poor. Perhaps those of us old sisters in retirement can do little else but pray that from the blood of these modern-day martyrs new vocations to a life of service may spring.

The Marist Sisters and the Religious of Jesus and Mary, who share life with us here at Marillac, have missions in developing countries where young people still heed the call to leave all and follow the Lord. It is in North America that few young people are entering religious life. Is the call now a universal call to an unreserved response to Christ's magnificent challenge to love God and neighbour as we love ourselves? Certainly, in our congregation the number of associates who share the responsibility of making love visible in today's world has risen dramatically. But does the power of religious life come from the power of community living?

Perhaps we are still in the process of renewal. We are still living the answers. The works of the Lord are mysterious. Our dying at this period of time is part of the mystery.

> Lo! I tell you a mystery. We shall not all sleep, but we shall all be changed, in a moment, in the twinkling of an eye, at the last trumpet....[W]e shall be changed. (I Cor. 15:51–52)

We are still being changed.

14

Atlantica Hotel

FROM AUGUST 20–23, 2016, WE Sisters of Charity, held our annual Assembly in Halifax at a hotel. We had no Motherhouse. Initially, I did not feel physically well enough to attend the Assembly. Old age was slowly creeping up on me. The waiting periods, the long walks, the security measures—all these factors had taken the joy out of air travel. I also felt that everything that could be said about issues in the congregation had already been said in former chapters and assemblies. The time of renewal was over; our ranks have steadily decreased from almost 1,700 to an elderly group of a little over 300. We are dying out and I was content to go out quietly, rejoicing that I played a part in the widespread expansion of Christian education in the nineteenth and twentieth centuries.

However, I did attend the Assembly of 2016, and for me the highlight of the event was the presentation of *Time of Trouble*, an opera by Elizabeth Raum with Libretto by Rex Deveux. The music, juxtaposing cacophonous, often jarring modern strains with the quiet serenity of ancient Gregorian chant, caught the turbulence of a chaotic time in our congregation's history. The libretto told the story of our almost extinction between 1880 and 1882, and made me aware that change has always been a constant of religious life. Although congregations are founded on spiritual principles, human nature always interferes.

The opera, focusing on the hostile ambivalence of the early years in our history, tells the story of Mother Mary Francis Maguire's refusal to accept Archbishop Michael Hannan's high-handed interference in the affairs of the community. She dared to question the extent of authority exercised by the Superior General, the Reverend Michael Hannan. It illustrated the conflicts that existed between the Sisters of Charity and the hierarchy of Halifax; between Mother Mary Francis, then Mother General, and Mother Elizabeth, the prior Mother General, and finally the conflict among the sisters themselves.

The opera proved to be a graced time for me, bringing me back to the earliest history of our community, to that period before our own "Troubles," to the time of our early Mothers who modelled such a strong combination of American-Canadian influences. In 1849, the first sisters sent from the New York Sisters of Charity to continue Vincent de Paul's work with the poor in the garrison town of Halifax, Nova Scotia, were four Americans: Sister Mary Basilia as Sister Servant (the original title for a Sister of Charity Superior), Sister Mary Cornelia, Sister Mary Rose and Sister Mary Vincent.

Sister Basilia McCann became the first Mother of the Halifax congregation, but she returned to the New York community in 1858, and was succeeded by Sister Rose McAleer, who, as Sister Francis d'Assisi McCarthy tells us, in her *A Trio of Mothers*, "was little prepared and ill-adapted by nature and temperament" to be an effective leader. Her election as Mother Superior "jeopardized the very existence of the young community."[17] Sister Mary Rose left the Halifax community and was not accepted back into the New York congregation. She then applied to the Sisters of Mercy and gained admission on condition that she go to California where she later died. The renowned Mother Basilia McCann, as well as the unknown and forgotten Sister Rose McAleer, form an integral part of our heritage.

Our first Canadian Superior was Mother Mary Josephine (Joanna Carroll), who was born in Nova Scotia in 1815. Hers was a late vocation. An experienced teacher, she entered the community in 1857, at the ripe old age of 42 and was elected Mother Superior in 1864. By this time the young community was expanding with missions in the French-speaking areas of Nova Scotia and New Brunswick. In *A Trio of Mothers*, Sister McCarthy wrote, "[I]n Mother Josephine Carroll the congregation was blessed with a woman who had everything: culture, experience, maturity and above all a proven, and practical piety."[18]

The second Canadian and the fourth Superior of the congregation was Mother Mary Elizabeth (Catherine O'Neill), born in Halifax in 1832. She entered the community on Palm Sunday, March 17, 1856, and on December 8, 1870, at the age of 38, she was elected to the office of Mother Superior. It was during her administration that we acquired the property at Rockingham and established the first Mount Saint Vincent, completed in 1873. It was also during her administration that the drama which provided the libretto of the opera the *Time of Trouble* started.

At this time, the young community of the Halifax Sisters of Charity had a kind and genial Superior General in the person of Archbishop Thomas Louis Connolly, a benefactor as well as a friend of the sisters. He died in 1876, and his successor was not appointed until 1877, during which time Mother Mary Elizabeth O'Neill's term had expired. She was succeeded by Mother Mary Francis (Mary Anne Maguire), but contrary to custom, Mother Elizabeth was not elected to a position on the general council. It was evident that there were different opinions regarding the sisters' visits to Archbishop Connolly's summer residence at Dutch Village. Mother Francis disapproved of her predecessor's (Mother Elizabeth O'Neill) freedom in allowing the sisters to entertain the Archbishop who was subject to depression. The music and frivolities were "worldly." In *A Trio of Mothers* Sister Francis d'Assisi McCarthy writes:

> 'Factions' is an ugly word in the apocrypha of a religious community, but one comes across the suggestion of it here. As yet it had not crystallized, and it is conceivable that at this point motivation was completely sincere and genuine. 'A certain weakness due to vanity,' to quote one who knew her well, had somehow blinded Mother M. Elizabeth to the imprudence of yielding always to Archbishop Connolly's mistaken kindness to the sisters. When the wiser ones among them had begged her to refuse invitations to the sisters to attend social functions at his summer house at Dutch Village, she compromised by going herself, as a sort of chaperon, apparently unaware that the vicar General of the Archdiocese [Dr. Hannan] was also disapproving of these affairs.[19]

From the serene, gentle rule of Mother Josephine Carroll and the light, relaxed governance of Mother Elizabeth O'Neill, the young community of the Sisters of Charity of Halifax went to the no nonsense leadership of Mother Mary Francis Maguire. Sister Francis d'Assisi describes her concisely: "She was a strict Superior, perhaps somewhat lacking in that Christlike gentleness which one hopes to find in religious leaders."[20] She was a reformer and a stern objector to the frivolities generated by Archbishop Connolly's kindness. In this matter she was likeminded to the newly elected Archbishop Michael Hannan, but her strength of character and administrative ability would be more than a match for Hannan's autocratic control.

At the height of the conflict between Archbishop Hannan and Mother Mary Francis Maguire, Mother Mary Francis and her council sent two sisters, Sister Mary de Sales Dwyer and Mary Aloysia Holden, to Rome to appeal our position before the Sacred Congregation for the Propagation of the Faith. The Sisters' cause was supported by powerful members of the laity, particularly by Sir John Thompson, a future Prime Minister of Canada. The final Decree, dated April 30, 1880, removed the sisters from the jurisdiction of Archbishop Hannan and placed them under the "immediate care" of Pope Leo XIII with jurisdiction to be exercised by Bishop Cameron. There was no Superior General.

New superiors would be called Mother General. From Sister Servant to Mother Superior to Mother General—the titles express the momentous change in authority in the thirty years between 1849 and 1880.

Fourteen of the sixty sisters left the community during the troubles. The community numbered less than forty at the end. However, once we came under the protection of Pope Leo XIII, these forty women became a "resurrected" community.

So, even at the historic Assembly of August, 2016, when we honestly faced our dying, there was a resurrection, an aura of new life and energy and a deeper appreciation of the Canadian input into the history of the congregation. Sometimes, we overlook this fact. We Americans pride ourselves on our vitality and robustness, but the *Time of Trouble* illustrated the power there is in quiet but dogged, polite determination. I hope we never lose the strong American/Canadian duality that is our heritage.

During the opera, I thought of another critical time in the history of religious life—an investigation by the same Sacred Congregation for the Propagation of the Faith into various religious congregations of sisters ministering to the People of God in the United States. The investigation centred on whether the changes made at the time of Vatican Council II had gone too far. Had these changes led to worldliness and a lessening of the importance of the vows on the part of modern religious? Were they adhering to strict Catholic teachings on moral issues? Were they obedient to the magisterium of the church? As the sisters were under fire, the laity, both Catholic and secular, played a significant role in the sisters' ultimate exoneration. There was a stunning show of support for the sisters and the contributions they had made to the people of the United States during the late nineteenth and twentieth centuries, particularly in the fields of education, health care and social work.

The two sisters sent to Rome were the quiet means by which our resurrection was accomplished. Mary de Sales Dwyer and Mary Aloysia Holden had been sent to Rome to defend the congregation from domination by a chauvinistic clergy. They were true pioneers. We know very little of these two sisters, but Sister Francis d'Assisi McCarthy tells us in her book *Two Mothers* that Mary de Sales had a "young, vibrant, cultured personality," that she spoke fluent French and that she was well-connected. Sister Aloysia, on the other hand, though not robust, had an attractive personality which was "appeal[ing] for lay people." Perhaps most significantly, Aloysia was a "personal friend" of Sir John and Mrs. Thompson "who had named one of their children in her honor."[21] These two first generation of Sisters of Charity were good exemplars of a vibrant, burgeoning congregation, whose members were "wise as serpents and innocent as doves" (Matt. 10:16).

Sisters Mary de Sales and Mary Aloysia witnessed a resurrection of the thirty-odd member community of the Sisters of Charity in Halifax. They had found the fullness of living the Christian life. They encapsulate the spirit of the congregation whose charism to make God's love visible in today's world, the charism that will be carried on by our Associates. I may not see that resurrection day, but I believe that future consecrated religious will find the same fullness of life that I found and witnessed to fifty years ago when I concluded *Nothing on Earth*.

And what is the fullness of Christian life? It is simply penetrating to the core of existence. It is seeing in nature, in the times we live in,

in people, in events, in our petty triumphs and our fertile failures –
not just creatures but the wheat grains that make up a living bread
over which Christ says, *"Hoc est enim Corpus Meum."* This is my life:
to contact God in everything, and then hold Him fast.

I'd be afraid to live for, by, and in myself alone. I'd be strangled
by my own conceit, starved by my own selfishness, and deceived by
my own treachery. That is why I left self behind to become a Sister
of Charity, that is why, too, my life is like *nothing on earth.*

15

A Long Postscript

It's November, the dying of the year, the great trees outside my windows have already shed half their leaves, but yet the sun streaming through the remaining yellow leaves bathes my morning world with light and hope. In a few hours I'll be attending the annual Mass of Remembrance in which the names of all those sisters and friends who have died during the past year are read to the sombre tolling of a bell. Of course I'll remember all my family members, most of whom have gone before me. I'll also remember Betty and Agatha, my dear friends who perished in the car accident.

I have mentioned in earlier pages that one of the questions that haunted me for years after the accident was, "Why was I saved and Agatha and Betty killed?" One answer to the question was that I, who had lived through the radical changes following Vatican II, might write this memoir, but there has also been a more personal reason. I want Agatha and Betty to be remembered with me because they had lived out those changes so effectively—more so than I had. We parted on that lonely, isolated road in New Brunswick, but I've carried the memory of their goodness with me over the years. In a matter of moments, all had been changed. The accident gave Agatha and Betty a new birth into the timelessness of eternity, and the accident wrought in me not only physical but also, more importantly, spiritual changes. I learned the prayer of silence. It was a type of resurrection. Something *could* come from nothing.

So, in the long months following the accident, when I felt that I was good for nothing, slowly but very clearly, I began to realize how completely Agatha and Betty had lived out the changes in religious life. I think now that the real reason why I was saved in the back seat of that Pontiac Sunbird was to memorialize the lives of two good Sisters of Charity: Sister Agatha Vienneau and Sister Elizabeth Bellefontaine. Like Aloysia and Mary de Sales who went to Rome to intercede for the little congregation at a time of near extinction, Agatha and Betty have gone to the Heavenly Jerusalem to intercede for us. Their lives are messages of simple yet profound goodness. They faithfully lived out the dictum of Vatican II's renewal to bring religious life into the modern world.

I've often regretted that I did not know more about Sisters Mary de Sales and Aloysia, but I do not want future Sisters of Charity to forget Agatha and Betty. I remember them daily in prayer, keep their photos on my dresser and now I offer a brief summary of their lives because both epitomized the holiness in the ordinary.

They were good Sisters for whom God was truly their All. I have tried to capture their goodness in two vignettes which I have added in a lengthy Postscript.

16

Sister Agatha Marie Vienneau

AGATHA MARIE VIENNEAU, BORN IN Bathurst, New Brunswick, on March 12, 1927, was the daughter of Theresa Barthilotte and John Joseph Vienneau. She was the second youngest of four children who lost their father when they were all very young. Agatha was not yet three when her father died. Perhaps the key to Agatha's personality rests with the early death of her father. She was an extremely affectionate child, but the father, suffering from tuberculosis, was afraid to let the child snuggle into his lap or to let himself get too close to his youngest daughter because of fear of infecting her. Often when she tried to climb upon her father's knee, he would send her away, unhugged and unkissed. This early rejection, gentle as it was and understood only later in life, left Agatha with a deep feeling of timidity. She never wanted people to hug or kiss her. She became a very private person.

Yet, despite her shyness and wariness of familiarity, Agatha was an extremely happy person. Her older brother Lionel remembers her as a child blessed with a sunny disposition. She was always ready to help her mother—except when it came to washing dishes!

Then Agatha always had something urgent to do elsewhere.

Another characteristic was her penchant to walk with a slight little tilt to her head, as if she were carefully scrutinizing everyone and everything, which indeed she was. Lionel recalls how, as children, Agatha would carefully watch when he would be away from home and then steal his bike. Of course, there would be a ruckus raised, but Agatha seemed not to mind her brother's ire.

The Vienneaus were an extremely close family. Her brothers liked to tease the naive Agatha who maintained a very devoted relationship with her brothers John and Lionel and with her older sister Agnes who was a surrogate mother to her when Mrs. Vienneau was forced to earn a livelihood for her fatherless young family. These were the dark years of the great depression, and in those days Canada did not have the excellent social services it has in place today. Then, there was neither governmental help for widows, nor insurance. Despite the financial hardships, perhaps because of them, the family members became very close, extremely devoted to each other. The mother worked as a housekeeper at the local presbytery and managed to keep her young family well clothed and well fed.

When Agatha was around six, she contracted scarlet fever and the entire family was placed under a strict quarantine. This event occurred just before Christmas and good Mrs. Vienneau was unable to do any shopping for the usual Christmas presents.

Imagine Agatha's surprise when she woke up on Christmas morning to find her bed covered with presents for everyone in the family! When Agatha asked where all the gifts came from, her mother quickly answered, "Santa Claus." If before the advent of her scarlet fever, the six-year-old child had any doubts about the existence of the roly-poly man in the red suit, she became a firm believer afterwards. In later years, she discovered that the real Santa Claus was the good family doctor, Dr. Dinsmore. The incident testifies not only to the closeness of the family bond, but also to that of the community. All her life, Agatha was to maintain a devoted love for her town of Bathurst, New Brunswick.

Ten years after the death of her husband, Mrs. Vienneau remarried. Agatha was now in her teens, and with World War II imminent, her brothers would soon be leaving home. Agatha was thirteen and Lionel seventeen when the latter joined the Air Force and became a pilot. Her younger brother John served in the Navy. When the mother re-married, two families were merged. The children of the step-father were much older and, perhaps resenting the younger family, left home soon after the marriage. In a sense, the war brought an end to Agatha's childhood. Both brothers returned from the war, attended university and started their own families. By this time, Agatha had entered the convent and had begun her career as a teacher. At the time of her death, only Lionel remained of that loving, close family. Now he too has gone.

In appearance, Agatha might be described as bonnie, with a fresh complexion, high colouring, laughing blue eyes and a ready smile. When I met her for the first time when we were postulants, she reminded me of the Campbell Soup Kid with her round face and merry countenance. I remember particularly one autumn Saturday afternoon when we postulants were allowed to go for a walk in the woods. We had just been introduced to the daily examination of conscience, and Agatha and I were comparing our predominant faults—something which we were counselled not to do. I confessed to pride and ambition. She acknowledged her jealousy. That little incident was one of the few instances of genuine sharing that I have ever experienced. I date the beginning of a friendship that spanned fifty-three years to that walk.

After our first profession of vows on April 17, 1949, Agatha was sent to St. Peter's School in Dartmouth, Nova Scotia. I went to Resurrection-Ascension School in Rego Park, New York. Agatha taught grade five and I started at grade three. We never lived together, only wrote sporadically throughout the years; but every time we got together for renewal of vows, perpetual profession, community meetings or congregational celebrations, Agatha and I would gravitate towards each other. Perhaps that was why we joined the same cluster. We could share fears and failures as well as hopes and successes. We could even gossip! But in all those years, I never heard Agatha utter a mean or unkind word. It was easy to share oneself with Agatha. She possessed a discerning mind with a keen desire to do everything well. She was open-hearted, unpretentious, non-threatening, always above board. Her basic honesty and ingenuousness were reflected in her smile. Somehow the sun seemed to shine brighter when Agatha smiled or, rather, her smile reflected the sun's open, honest light. She loved the open air. Walking Bathurst's three bridges in the early morning light and tending her garden were her chief delights. The earth with its flowers, the sky with its early morning stars, the sea with its calm and its rage—these were the food of her contemplation. Their beauty and power were not wasted on her soul. But as open as was her countenance and as merry as her smile to friends and neighbours, Agatha preferred the privacy of solitude. That is why walking by herself or working alone in her garden gave her such intense pleasure.

But the basis of Agatha's spirituality can be traced back to her devotion to St. Therese de Lisieux whose "little way" to holiness became Agatha's own. Before leaving the postulate for the novitiate, each of us candidates for religious vows was allowed to submit three names by which we would thenceforth be known.

Agatha's first choice for her religious name was Sister Robert Therese. Unknown to her, another sister in the group also had asked for that name. The Postulant Mistress, in an unheard of move, asked the latter if she would consider another name as Miss Vienneau had also requested that name. I don't think Agatha ever knew of this incident, and I only knew of it when I came to write this little testament, but it reveals Agatha's natural charm, her quiet ability to draw others to herself because of her unassuming nature. No great deeds did Agatha perform. She was never made a superior or elected to any high religious office. Her greatest challenges (and successes) came from her inner life.

Through fidelity to prayer, Agatha grew in self-knowledge and self-acceptance, which were the bedrock of her honesty. From her earliest novitiate days, when the daily examen of conscience was instilled into us, Agatha never abandoned her quest for self-understanding. Her humility was grounded in a principle to which she would always return: love God, avoid evil, begin again and again and again that search for insight into the self, for acceptance of one's weaknesses as well as one's strengths.

Agatha also grew in gratitude. Thanksgiving might well have been her deepest expression of her love—thanksgiving and vigilance in accepting what God wanted in the present circumstances of her life. Sometimes God led where she did not want to follow, but, like her patroness St. Therese, she went because she trusted in her God's steadfast love.

When I try to fathom why I was saved and dear Agatha and Betty were taken, my clearest answers, and my bulwark against despair comes in the psalms. Prayer has taken on a whole new meaning, and the psalms come alive as never before. I remember reading: "I shall not die,/ I shall live.../and recount his deeds:/ I was punished, I was punished by the Lord,/ but not doomed to die" (Psalm 18:36–49). I was not "doomed to die" because, if I lived, I could recount the goodness of God to Agatha and her response to that goodness by her little way of accepting herself and of serving others. I could recount her goodness to her pupils; her kindness, her joy in bringing them into music festivals and even winning prizes; her retirement days when she served meals on wheels to the elderly; her generosity of spirit even offering to take over the driving five minutes before she died because I had "driven too long" and "must be tired." Service was one of the hallmarks of Agatha's little way.

Our congregational symbol presents the cross and with it the basin and towel representing Christ's loving service in washing his disciples' feet. Agatha's discipleship was seen in her living out the spirit and mission of our congregation, which states very succinctly: "We Sisters of Charity of Saint Vincent de Paul, are a congregation of consecrated women sharing the gift of a call to give joyful witness to love: the love of God, of one another and of all persons" (*Constitutions* 1). That "giving joyful witness to love" took several forms—like feeding the homeless who came to Sacred Heart Convent. I happened to be visiting her once when I was given a perfect example of her devotion. We were having a late night cup of tea in the kitchen when there was a loud knock at the door. Agatha opened it to a gangly adolescent who explained that he had left home and had only enough money to get him to Halifax. The lad hadn't eaten all day. Agatha went about packing a huge lunch of sandwiches, cookies and Coke. She did it so effortlessly that I knew hers was a practiced hand. Her Eucharist that night was her miracle of love. With Agatha, everyone was welcome at her table of the Lord. She gave food and she gave love to those in most need of it.

One of her friends was a mentally challenged woman whom, for purposes of anonymity, I'll call Phyllis. Every Tuesday, without fail, Phyllis would visit Agatha who would make a special lunch for her friend and then play two or three games of Scrabble with her. It was the highlight of Phyllis' week and a commitment that Agatha religiously kept. The mayor's or governor's wife would not have been treated more royally than was Phyllis.

Her sister-in-law Jeannine considered Agatha her best friend and attested to her capacity to listen and to comfort. Because Agatha possessed an intensely spiritual life, she was an extraordinarily good listener. In one year Jeannine had lost two members of her family and she would tell of the comfort she received at her kitchen table when Agatha and she would talk for hours about their bereavements. By that time Agatha, too, had lost her beloved sister Agnes at the age of fifty-four and her cherished brother John, aged sixty-seven. In one of these conversations with Jeannine, Agatha confided that she never expected to live beyond her seventieth year.

In reflecting on Agatha after her death, Jeannine remembered how she had told Agatha that she did not like to stay alone, and when her husband Lionel became ill and had to be hospitalized, Agatha came from Bathurst to Edmonston to stay with her. It was to be Agatha's last visit. After a very difficult operation, Lionel was sent home from the hospital too early. His incision opened; he bled profusely, and Jeannine had to rush him to the hospital immediately. The bathroom was covered with blood, but when Jeannine returned from the hospital, she was greeted by an exceedingly pale Agatha. Agatha, who hated the sight of blood, had scoured the bathroom to pristine cleanliness. Love of one's neighbor takes many different forms of service.

But it is not her active sharing of love for which I am most indebted to Agatha. She taught me more by her quiet little way of achieving companionship with her Maker in solitude. Her solitude, however, was not without its difficulties. Has it ever been easy really to face the self? To accept oneself? Few of us ever accept ourselves as others know us. Ever since that first earnest conversation I had with Agatha wherein she acknowledged her jealousy, and I, my pride and ambition, Agatha had to struggle for self-acceptance. More than anyone I know, Agatha saw the absurdity of the self, its irrationality, its confusing contradictions. Sometimes I feel that Agatha's love of order, her care in dressing, her love of beauty and of the proper arrangement of things were reactions to the confusion she found in herself. But because she accepted the infirmities in her own make-up, she could be patient with the character defects, the temperamental failings of others. If ever we discussed the faults of others (and we did, *mea culpa*), she could always laugh and make me laugh too at our human absurdities.

Agatha's humility was the wellspring of her little way to union with God. Her major challenge to holiness (or wholeness) came from her knowledge of her dissatisfaction with the self. She did not ignore the reality; she had no illusions about herself. Yet, Agatha's wonderful charm came from its paradoxical nature. In all her wrestlings with self-negation, she never lost sight of her God given potential, the limitlessness of her ideals, her basic right to be an individual, a part of God's wonderful earth. Hers was not a servile, death-dealing humility, but a glorious acceptance of herself as she was—perhaps a little too chubby, a little too sensitive. She knew she was precious in God's sight. That is why Agatha's garden was her chief delight. There her magnificent flowers, so brilliantly varied, rose from the naked, black soil and would return to that ever-changing compound of birth, brilliance, decay, and death. She knew she was allowed the limitless promise of the earth and gloried in that infinite potential. And so, in her inner solitude, in the spiritual garden of prayer, in her day-by-day working out of the weeds and crab grass of her personality, she found self-acceptance and a wonderful peace that was so easily discerned in her smile.

In our last meeting, a month before the accident, we were on Cape Cod for the band reunion of our golden jubilee year, and one morning at breakfast, Agatha reported that she was awakened during the night by a loud knocking at her door. She got up, but no one was there. One other sister also heard the knocking. Later that day, Agatha received a telephone message that her older step sister had died. Agatha took the knocking as a premonition.

Another time Agatha told me that one morning, after John's death, when she was taking her usual walk over Bathurst's three bridges, she saw John passing in an automobile. He was smiling and waving. She took the incident as an omen that she was not to mourn for him. He was happy and at peace. By the end of her life, I think the unseen world had become very real to Sister Agatha Vienneau.

Agatha's gift of interior solitude enabled her to take responsibility for her own life of faith. Over the fifty years of her religious life, she faced the mystery of her own being and fought the lonely, barely comprehensible task of working her way through the darkness of her own mysterious self. She understood Christ's prayer in Gethsemane, his fear and his courage: "If it be possible, let this Chalice pass. . .but not my will but thine be done!" She heard Christ's voice in the midst of her own suffering: "Fear not ... it is I," and she knew that somehow, someway, she was *becoming* Christ. She found comfort in recognizing that the mystery of her self was part of the mystery of God, and she became lost in the wonder of that glorious mystery. By the end of her life, Agatha possessed the true gift of contemplation. She was a woman truly at peace with herself. Hers was a joyful, calm tranquillity.

In that long walk and conversation that I had with Agatha about a month before the accident, she told me jokingly of another eerie premonition she recently had been given. It seems that a local nun, Sister Therese Vienneau, had been killed in a car crash. The convent where Agatha lived was besieged with telephone calls, Mass cards, flowers, and many other tributes. The good people of Bathurst confused Sister Therese Vienneau with Sister Robert Therese Vienneau (Agatha's religious name). She was given a preview of the affection in which she had been held, and she was astounded by the love which this case of mistaken identity revealed. The genuineness of people's affection for her would be acknowledged within a very few weeks.

Agatha had not realized that she had truly lived out St. Therese's little way. She had become very comfortable in her unseen world. A true solitary, despite the many friends she had both in the community and outside of it, she held firmly to that sense of aloneness. That is why it seems so strange that Agatha had a companion in death. In the supreme moment of solitude, she was not alone. Although she and Betty died side by side, it is impossible to measure the time that separated their passing.

Whatever happens in those minutes, those seconds after death, I sometimes picture Agatha and Betty exchanging views, finding something to laugh about, perhaps commenting about what was happening at the accident scene, but all the time Agatha (and Betty too) would hold on to her own solitude.

Certainly, when I relive the tragedy of my sisters' deaths, and try to find meaning in the chaos of those last moments and the seemingly incomprehensible way in which life went on after their deaths—their personal effects given away; their clothes distributed to the poor; the apparent forgetfulness that settles in as the weeks and months pass—I think of St. Therese's little way and Agatha's own little way, her vocation to love. She did the simple love-filled actions that came to hand day after day; she prayed faithfully and lived a faith-filled, hidden life in solitude. Her attention to life's simple events was captured in her expert photography. Whatever the occasion, Agatha had her camera ready to catch the joy of the moment. As a photographer, she was usually outside the picture. Lionel's wife, Jeanine, attested to what these pictures meant to her and to the family: "We will always remember Agatha and her camera. She took snaps of every event and everyone. Sister Paule sent us a big box full of albums, which we go through every time one of our children comes for a visit. We will miss her—for her humour, her devotion and her love of children."

We all miss Agatha. Sr. Paule Cantin gave fitting witness to Agatha's life in her beautiful homily, delivered on the day of her funeral. And how Agatha would have laughed at the anomalies of that funeral. She, who didn't want any celebration for her jubilee, she, who possessed such a remarkable degree of humility, was given a magnificent farewell. A bishop and five priests celebrated at the altar; the day was vintage October with trees waving their red and gold leaves in the sunlight. As the body was being carried from the church, the rousing cries of laughing children at their morning play period rinsed the air. Agatha was laid to rest amid sunshine and laughter. She must have been smiling.

17

Sister Elizabeth Bellefontaine

THERE IS SOMETHING SIMILAR BETWEEN the Lord's call to Samuel and that to Margaret Elizabeth Bellefontaine. Both were called very young and both had parents who left their children at a very early age. Hannah, the mother of Samuel, after being barren until old age, vowed to give her child to the Lord for service in the temple if she could conceive. When he passed his infancy, Samuel was given into the care of Eli. Margaret, the mother of Elizabeth, died at the early age of 24; her husband was to follow her in another three years. Their two children, Edward (Ted), six, and Elizabeth (Betty), four, were left to the care of a beloved grandaunt.

Orphaned at such an early age, an intensely devoted bond existed between sister and brother. Remembering his sister, Ted wrote that Betty was born on September 1, 1934 in her grandfather's house on Quinpool Road in Halifax, Nova Scotia. He wrote, "When Betty was one-year old, we moved to Fairview, and not long afterwards, my mother passed away on November 10, 1937. At that time, Betty was only three years old and I was five. My father took Betty and me back to Quinpool Road to live with my grandfather and my grandaunt. Our grandfather's name was

William Bishop and our aunt's name was Maude Brunt, known more affectionately as 'Mum Brunt.' Mum had no children of her own; her husband was killed in World War I shortly after they were married."

The seeds of Betty's avid love for Canada were planted by her grandaunt who never forgot her young husband and the sacrifice he made for Canada. Ted was to make his primary career in the Canadian navy, and Betty had a deep love of country and especially for the men and women in the armed forces. She would never let an Armistice Day pass without wearing her poppy, keeping silence at 11 o'clock and watching the national commemorative service on television. She also possessed a deep love for Halifax, the city of her birth. She knew every nook and cranny of the city, especially the Public Gardens and the Commons, and she genuinely loved Halifax's traditions and its colourful history.

Betty's maternal grandmother had died of a ruptured appendix when she was only twenty-three and her sister Maude (Mum) took over the task of raising Betty and Ted's mother as well as another brother and sister. When the young Mr. Bellefontaine died of tuberculosis, on April 8, 1940, Mum Brunt took over the care of the children, Ted, now seven and Betty, five. Mum Brunt was then in her fifties and she had already raised one family. Of the beloved Mum and Grandpa Bishop, Ted wrote, "We couldn't have gotten more love than if they were our own parents." Ted and Betty considered themselves the sole survivors of their family; no wonder Ted confessed, "When Betty was killed in that car accident, I felt as if half of my body was cut off."

Before he died, Betty's father had begged the sisters at the Oxford Street School in Halifax to allow his daughter to begin her schooling even though she was only five years old and six was the mandated starting age. Also before he died, the young Mr. Bellefontaine told Grandfather Bishop that he wanted Betty and Ted to be placed in Joseph's Orphanage, run by the Sisters of Charity, since he himself had been placed there when he was a young boy, and he considered those years the happiest of his life. However, Mum Brunt and Grandfather Bishop did not think that decision was a wise one, because the children might eventually be split up for adoption. The grandfather and aunt decided that the children would remain with them.

Even though the children remained with their relatives on Quinpool Road, they still came under the welfare department whose only contribution at that time was eight pints of milk a week. Welfare's interference was indeed minimal, but since both the children's parents had died of tuberculosis, they had to attend the public clinic twice each year for what was then called a Fluoroscope. At one of these sessions, it was discovered that Betty had a spot on her lung that had not healed. As a result, she was forced to miss two months of school. This loss of school at such a critical time put Betty behind and made her feel inferior to some of her classmates. She used to say that she was a bit of a dummy until she reached the seventh grade. Then she had a mental awakening and from that moment on there was no holding her back. For the rest of her school life, Betty was always recommended, which meant that she did not have to write final examinations.

There was an unusual affinity between Ted and Betty. All through childhood Betty and Ted looked out for each other's interests. Since both children were on welfare until they were sixteen, they were forced to attend for two weeks in the summer a camp called Rainbow Haven, located at Cow Bay, Nova Scotia. It was supposed to be a fun place allowing orphaned children to get out of the city. For Betty and Ted, however, it was more like a concentration camp, and they counted the days until the bus came to take them home. Betty was only five when they went to camp for the first time and her only memory was her having those summer play suits that had the bottom buttoned to the top. She could never get the buttons undone by herself and several times, when she had to go to the bathroom, she had an "accident" because there was nobody around to help her with the buttons. Betty was sentenced to Rainbow Haven twice. After that Grandpa Bishop and their beloved Mum managed to obtain reprieves for both children.

When she was about six years old, Ted was made to take Betty with him to the movies on Saturdays. One day they had to sit in the very first row of the theatre when the movie playing was Frankenstein. Betty was terrified at the sight of the monster.

She began yelling, "Take me home! Take me home or I'll tell Mum on you." Ted took her out, saw that she was safely across the street and then went back into the movie. Even if he had not taken her home, the two children would have been thrown out because, as Ted remembers, "No one could hear what was going on with her yelling at me."

When she was about eleven, one of Ted's friends got a new cart, and the neighbourhood children, including Betty, were taking turns riding in the cart while the rest of the youngsters pushed and pulled the rider up and down the street. When it came to Betty's turn for a ride, the owner of the cart told her she could not have a ride. Even then, wrote Ted, "she could 'diplomatically' solve a dispute, so, without saying a word, but using an unusually good right cross for a girl, she solved the problem and got her ride."

At sixteen, Betty graduated from Saint Patrick's High School in Halifax as class valedictorian, and three months later she entered the congregation of the Sisters of Charity. Ted had entered the Royal Canadian Navy at that time, and Betty wrote to her brother asking him what he thought about her entering the sisterhood.

Betty was acutely conscious that she loved dancing, new clothes and life in general. She used to relate how on Saturdays she would work at the local bakery, and when the shop closed at nine, she would run home and get dressed for the CYO dances in the parish church hall. Betty was very conscious of what she was giving up when she entered the convent; so her request to Ted for some advice might have been a simple ploy for a delay in her decision making. But her brother replied that, since he had made up his own mind about entering the navy, it was up to her to decide what was best for her. Her appeal for approval from her "big" brother (Ted was just nineteen at the time) reveals once again the closeness between the two siblings.

After she entered the convent, Elizabeth Bellefontaine, then called Sister Margaret Elizabeth, developed a very distinct brand of spirituality. It was not the "Imitation" of Christ that drew Betty, for how could she possibly imitate a man who had been dead for almost two thousand years? What aspect of his unknown personality could she possibly imitate? Betty found her answer in Christ's obedience to the Father's will. If left to her own choice, Betty would have preferred having parents who lived to see their children established in life. That was not to be. In the very fact of her own loss, Betty established her strong faith in the liberating power of God's will. It was to be the hallmark of her intense spirituality—obedience to the Father's will, obedience to what is! But it was a joyful obedience. Betty could discover some element of humour in every event.

After her three years of postulate and novitiate training, Betty made her profession as a Sister of Charity, and in September of 1954, she began her teaching career in a grade one classroom at St. Stephen's School in Halifax. Whether at home in the convent or in the school, Betty could see the humour in the ordinary situations of life. One day she took aside a little boy who was constantly inattentive in class. The young nun and the little boy had a private heart-to-heart talk. Never did Sister Margaret Elizabeth look down on her pupils; rather, she delighted in talking to her young charges as adults. So she began to lecture the little six-year-old: "I cannot comprehend why you continue to misconstrue the object of your painstaking intellectual endeavours. Furthermore, you perpetuate the complication of matters by alienating yourself from your confreres." Then the punch line: "Do you understand what I've been trying to communicate to you?" The little lad, at no loss for an answer, replied: "My mommy told me what it all means, but I forgot."

On another occasion, in her early years at Saint Stephen's, Betty was helping the cook in the kitchen. The sister-in-charge had her wash and cut up the chicken they were having for supper, then put the pieces into the sauce that was on the stove. As Betty stirred the chicken in the sauce, it seemed to be getting so stiff that she could not move the wooden spoon. She called the cook who discovered that instead of sauce, Betty had put the chicken into a pot of starch meant for stiffening the nuns' collars and coifs. Without telling anyone, they rescued the chicken from the starch, washed the pieces and placed them into the proper pot.

None of the sisters who enjoyed their supper that night ever knew the story of the starched chicken, only the cook, Betty and now you.

Even in these early years, Betty did the unpleasant tasks silently, without comment, without fuss. She knew what the Lord was doing when He washed the feet of his disciples. During her first year as a professed Sister of Charity, there was an old sister in the convent who was very ill and needed constant attention. Betty's duty was to empty sister's bedpan at 5:20 in the morning, before the community assembled for morning prayers. Although she had to get up earlier than the usual 5 a.m. rising and was revolted by the charge, she did it for months without fuss and without complaining.

After Ted had joined the navy, Betty and he only managed to see each other once a year when Ted was on leave. When he returned from duty in Korea, he received permission to visit Betty at any time in the week. After he was married, Ted was accompanied by his young wife Patricia who became a genuine sister to Betty. Pat recalled the first visit in 1958 when Betty was at Saint Stephen's Convent in Halifax. When they arrived, there were about fifty sisters at the door waiting to see the new baby, Brenda, who was then six weeks old. Pat, the new mother, was just twenty years old

and a recent convert to Catholicism. She was very nervous on her
first visit to a convent. It seemed like eternity before Betty came
down to join them. At that time, Betty was not allowed to visit
them alone or to eat with them. On that first visit, the young Mr.
and Mrs. Bellefontaine had dinner in the convent. Pat remembered
how Betty just sat there while they ate and it seemed very hard to
get to know her. But later, when Betty was allowed to come to their
home, Betty and Pat became very close. Pat also reminisced how,
although Betty was unusually jovial, she was a very private person,
but one who "helped me with my problems."

After years as a primary school teacher, Betty, who had already
earned B.A. and M.A. degrees, began studies for her doctorate.
Ted, now stationed out west, recalled that every time he had leave
in Halifax, Betty was either going to Saint Mary's College, Indiana
or to Notre Dame University. She had been a natural student from
her junior high school years, loving the hours of solitude that study
afforded, but she was never pompous or arrogant about her advanced
degrees. Her particular field of study for her doctorate was the
concept of law in the Old Testament. One sister remarked that in
her explanation of law and of scripture, Betty was simple and direct.
The law was made to protect freedom; it was never meant to bind
or to enslave.

After Betty finished her doctorate, she became an Assistant
Professor in the Religious Studies department at Mount Saint
Vincent University, where she would remain for almost thirty years.
Here she was known for her unusual dedication to her students,
spending hours in after-class tutorials and counselling sessions. She
was also very involved in committee work, and anyone working with
her on academic committees would soon realize the thoroughness
with which she read reports and minutes of meetings. But for all
her committee work, Betty also found time for scriptural research
and publication. Before she left The Mount, Betty was granted her
full professorship.

But it was as a councillor on the congregational leadership team that Betty Bellefontaine found her true calling. Intuitively, Betty seemed to realize that she was in touch with the silent needs, the needs that few speak of but are very, very real. She truly gave herself to her sisters. One night, Betty was late for supper, and I said, "You're late. If I heat up your dinner in the microwave, it will be too dry. Where were you?" "Oh," she replied, not the least bit concerned about her dried-up chicken, "Sister Mary X is in the hospital and asked me to clean her apartment because she is going to be there longer than she expected. It was a messy job!" I proceeded to heat her dinner, but I knew that Betty had done a very unpleasant job and did it lightly without much comment.

Even before she became a member of the congregation's administrative team, Betty thought of the forgotten ones. A sister told me how she had been under treatment at a substance abuse centre and Betty, when passing through Toronto, made it a point to visit her even though her time was limited. "I was really touched by that visit. After I recovered she was always ready to hear how I was doing over the years. That meant a lot to me." Another sister had the following memory of Betty:

> I needed a letter of recommendation from a higher superior in order to become certified as a chaplain. She wrote that letter with great thought and care. Throughout my time in CPE, she had called me periodically to see how I was surviving the process, and I really appreciated that concern, since I had not known her very well prior to her election to the team. I felt that she was really interested in me personally, apart from her job. To me she was a great gift for others. When she died, I felt a terrible void in my life, even though our connection had been very brief.

Sister after sister could recount stories of Betty's interest in them. Relatives and friends could also recall Betty's personal involvement with them as an individual. On the eve of her funeral, amidst stories of her scholarship, her attention to detail, her gift as a raconteur of jokes and stories, an obscure relative remarked that he did not know Betty as an academic or as a religious but simply as a good Christian. He told how a niece of his had become hopelessly involved in drugs and was living in squalid conditions. He admitted that few people would dare to go to the section of the city where the woman was living. Betty went, and went again and again, until the woman finally died, comforted by someone who simply cared.

God alone filled Sister Elizabeth Bellefontaine's heart. She sincerely tried to remain, by word and deed, faithful to God's presence within her. She walked with Jesus who was Love made visible. But love is growth, and by the end of her life, Betty found a joyful fulfilment in her role as a congregational leader. Because she believed in God's love for her, she moved from finding joy in God to giving joy to God by service done for others.

I have lived with very good women. I witnessed their youthful generosity and enthusiasm, the wisdom that came from failure, the living faith that kept them praying. May all my dear sisters, especially Agatha and Betty, rest in peace, and may their memory endure.

18

L'Envoi

I SEND THIS "SEQUEL" AND its Postscript on its way. It is a brief history, very brief, just a little over one hundred pages of the lives of three Sisters of Charity, but it is enough. The sequel begins its journey when I pass these pages on to Sister Joan O'Keefe, our congregational leader, whose favourite word seems to be *enough*. Joan will decide what to do with them.

It is *enough* that I have tried to record a personal experience of the changes that challenged religious congregations after the Vatican II Council. At first, I thought these changes would have little effect on my own stubborn views of religious life as I recorded them in *Nothing on Earth*. I accepted the *how* of the changes but not the *why*. I hope this sequel will make other souls more aware of the necessity of change in any era and, more importantly, of the necessity of prayer in our religious life.

What a mysterious word is *enough*. Even the phonetics of the word: the guttural *g*, the hissing *h*, the nullifying *n*, provoke the bulwarking effect of the consonants, stabilized by the moderating vowels, *a*, *o* and *u*. It is an intriguing word.

What is *enough*? In his poem "October" from *The Earthly Paradise*,

William Morris complained because he did not have "enough" of life and love, and just before she succumbed to death from cancer, my sister Evelyn lamented, "Enough is enough." Enough conveys the satisfaction of wants and needs. I am satisfied that I have shown how the changes initiated at Vatican II deepened my prayer life and satisfied my wants and needs. Prayer is everything and everything is prayer. I have found the God within. That is enough—more than enough.

The greatest grace from the Assembly of 2016 was that we honestly faced our dying. That was evident after we experienced the opera *Time of Trouble*. At that sacred meeting, there was a Resurrection, an aura of fresh life and energy, an expectation of something new arising. Only God knows what the future holds for the Sisters of Charity of Halifax. But no matter what form the congregation takes, may it never lose its blessed Vincentian spirit "to show forth the love of God by serving those in need" (*Constitutions* 4), or, as we express that charism today, "making God's love visible in today's world."

November 9, 2016

Notes

1. All of the biblical quotations in this book are from the Revised Standard Edition (New York, Glasgow, London: Collins, 1973).

2. Sandra M. Schneiders, IHM, *Finding the Treasure: Locating Catholic Religious Life New Ecclesial and Cultural Context* (Mahwah, NJ: Paulist Press, 2000), 126.

3. Sister Mary Olga McKenna, *Charity Alive: Sisters of Charity of Saint Vincent de Paul, Halifax, 1950-1980* (Lanham, MD: University Press of America, 1998), 194.

4. Ibid., 158.

5. Sister Joan D. Chittister, *The Fire in These Ashes: A Spirituality of Contemporary Religious Life* (Franklin, WI: Sheed & Ward, 1995), 169.

6. Thomas Gisborne, *An Inquiry into the Duties of the Female Sex* (London: Cadell & Davies, 1813), 7.

7. Ignatius, *Spiritual Exercises of St. Ignatius*, trans. and ed. Louis J. Puhl (Westminster, MD: Newman, 1963), 6.

8. John Milton, *Paradise Lost*, bk. 1, line 1263.

9. Martha Westwater, *The Wilson Sisters: A Biographical Study of Upper Middle Class Victorian Life* (Athens: OH: University Press, 1984).

10. Martha Westwater, *The Spasmodic Career of Sydney Dobell* (Lanham, MD: University Press of America, 1992).

11. Martha Westwater, *Giant Despair Meets Hopeful: Kristevan Readings in Adolescent Fiction* (Edmonton, AB: University of Alberta Press, 2000).

12. Julia Kristeva, *"The Adolescent Novel" in Abjection, Melancholia, and Love: The Work of Julia Kristeva,* eds. John Fletcher and Andrew Benjamin (London and New York, Routledge, 1990), 8.

13. William Shakespeare, *King Lear* Act I, scene ii, lines 21-22.

14. Gerald Manley Hopkins, *"The Wreck of the Deutschland,"* lines 1-4.

15. Sister Donna Geernaert, *The New Cosmology and Christian Faith,* (Halifax, Nova Scotia: Sisters of Charity, 2013), 2.

16. Ibid., 9.

17. Sister Francis d'Assisi McCarthy, *A Trio of Mothers: Mother Mary Rose McAleer; Mother Mary Josephine Carroll; Mother Mary Elizabeth O'Neill.* (Halifax, Nova Scotia: Mount Saint Vincent, 1968), 12.

18. Ibid., 46.

19. Ibid., 61.

20. Sister Francis d'Assisi McCarthy, *Two Mothers: M. Mary Francis McGuire; Mother Mary Benedicta Harrington* (Mount Saint Vincent, Halifax, Nova Scotia, 1971), 15.

21. Ibid., 42.

Printed in the United States
By Bookmasters